JOHN WESLEY'S
JOURNAL

First Edition, *September* 1902
Reprinted, *October* 1902

JOHN WESLEY'S JOURNAL

ABRIDGED BY

PERCY LIVINGSTONE PARKER

WITH

AN INTRODUCTION

BY

HUGH PRICE HUGHES, M.A.

AND AN

APPRECIATION OF THE JOURNAL

BY

AUGUSTINE BIRRELL, K.C.

LONDON

ISBISTER AND COMPANY, LIMITED

15 TAVISTOCK STREET, COVENT GARDEN

1902

Printed by BALLANTYNE, HANSON & CO.
London & Edinburgh

EDITOR'S NOTE

WHEN John Wesley prepared his Journal for publication he prefaced it with the following account of its origin :

"*It was in pursuance of an advice given by Bishop Taylor, in his 'Rules for Holy Living and Dying,' that, about fifteen years ago, I began to take a more exact account than I had done before, of the manner wherein I spent my time, writing down how I had employed every hour.*

"*This I continued to do, wherever I was, till the time of my leaving England for Georgia. The variety of scenes which I then passed through induced me to transcribe, from time to time, the more material parts of my diary, adding here and there such little reflections as occurred to my mind.*

"*Of this Journal thus occasionally compiled, the following is a short extract : it not being my design to relate all those particulars which I wrote for my own use only, and which would answer no valuable end to others, however important they were to me.*"

Rev. John Telford, one of Wesley's biographers, says that "*the earlier parts of the Journal were published in the interest of Methodism, that the calumny and slander then rife might be silenced by a plain narrative of the facts as to its founding, and its purpose. The complete Journals, still preserved in twenty-six bound volumes, have never been printed. Copious extracts were made by Wesley himself, and issued in twenty-one parts, the successive instalments being eagerly expected by a host of readers.*"

The published Journal makes four volumes, each about the size of the present book. But though I have had to curtail it by three-quarters I have tried to retain the atmosphere of tremendous activity which is one of its most remarkable features.

Mr. Birrell, in his " Appreciation," has focused in a very striking way the interest, actuality, and charm of Wesley's Journal, and all I have had to do was to select those portions which best illustrate them.

The wonder is that it has not been done before. Edward FitzGerald once wrote to Professor Norton, " Had I any interest with publishers I would get them to reprint parts of it," for he was a great lover of the Journal.

Writing to another friend about Wesley's " Journal," FitzGerald said, " If you don't know it, do know it. It is curious to think of this diary running coevally with Walpole's letters—diary—the two men born and dying too within a few miles of one another, and with such different lives to record. And it is remarkable to read pure, unaffected, undying English, while Addison and Johnson are tainted with a style which all the world imitated."

Macaulay's estimate of Wesley may also be recalled. Wesley, he said, was " a man whose eloquence and logical acuteness might have made him eminent in literature, whose genius for government was not inferior to that of Richelieu, and who, whatever his errors may have been, devoted all his powers in defiance of obloquy and derision, to what he sincerely considered as the highest good of his species."

Wesley is one of the most strenuous ethical figures in history, and literature has no other such record of personal endeavour as that contained in these pages. To make that record accessible to every one is the object of this edition.

INTRODUCTION

BY THE REV. HUGH PRICE HUGHES, M.A.

HE who desires to understand the real history of the English people during the seventeenth, eighteenth and nineteenth centuries should read most carefully three books: George Fox's " Journal," John Wesley's " Journal," and John Henry Newman's "Apologia pro Vitâ Suâ."

As Lord Hugh Cecil has recently said in a memorable speech, the Religious Question cannot be ignored. It is *the* Question; in the deepest sense it is the only Question. It has always determined the course of history everywhere. In all ages the sceptical literary class has tried to ignore it, as the Roman historians, poets, and philosophers ignored Christianity until the time when Christianity became triumphant and dominant throughout the Roman Empire.

But, however much ignored or boycotted by literary men, the growth or decline of religion ultimately settles everything. Has not Carlyle said that George Fox making his own clothes is the most remarkable event in our history? George Fox was the very incarnation of that Individualism which has played, and will yet play, so great a part in the making of modern England. If you want to understand " the dissidence of Dissent and

the Protestantism of the Protestant religion," read the
Journal of George Fox.

Then came John Wesley and his "helpers." They
were the first preachers since the days of the Franciscan
friars in the Middle Ages who ever reached the working
classes. In England, as in France, Germany, and everywhere else, the Reformation was essentially a middle-
class movement. It never captured either the upper
classes or the working classes. That explains its
limitations.

As Dr. Rigg has shown, Wesley's itineraries were
deliberately planned to bring him into direct contact
neither with the aristocracy nor with the dependent or
poverty-stricken poor, but with the industrious self-
supporting workmen in town and country. The ultimate
result was that " the man in the street " became Methodist
in his conception of Christianity, whatever his personal
conduct and character might be. A profound French
critic said, fifty years ago, that modern England was
Methodist, and the remark applies equally to the United
States and to our colonies. The doctrines of the
Evangelical Revival permeated the English-speaking
world.

Then Newman appeared on the scene and a tremendous change began. The Anglican Church revived, and
revived in Newman's direction. We witness to-day on
every side the vast results of the Newman era. Many of
these results are beneficial in the extreme ; others cannot
be welcome to those who belong to the schools of George
Fox and John Wesley.

The whole future of the British Empire depends upon
this question of questions—Will George Fox and John
Wesley on the one hand, or John Henry Newman on
the other, ultimately prevail ?   And the best way to

arrive at the true inwardness of the issue is to read, ponder, and inwardly digest Wesley's " Journal " and Newman's " Apologia."

It is a great advantage that Mr. Parker has secured permission to republish Mr. Augustine Birrell's " Appreciation." That brilliant writer demonstrates, that there is no book in existence that gives you so exact and vivid a description of the eighteenth century in England as Wesley's " Journal." It is an incalculably more varied and complete account of the condition of the people of England than Boswell's " Johnson." As Mr. Birrell says, Wesley was himself " the greatest force of the eighteenth century in England. No man lived nearer the centre than John Wesley. Neither Clive nor Pitt, neither Mansfield nor Johnson. No single figure influenced so many minds, no single voice touched so many hearts. No other man did such a life's work for England." Wesley has demonstrated that a true prophet of God has more influence than all the politicians and soldiers and millionaires put together. He is the incalculable and unexpected element that is always putting all the devices of the clever to naught.

I do not understand what Mr. Birrell means by saying that " as a writer Wesley has not achieved distinction. He was no Athanasius, no Augustine ; he was ever a preacher." It is true that Wesley's main business was not to define metaphysical theology, but to cultivate friendly relations with Christians of all schools, and to save living men from sin. But he gave a death-blow to the destructive dogma of limited salvation with which the names of Augustine and Calvin will be for ever associated.

No doubt, like Oliver Cromwell, Wesley was essentially

a " man of action," and he deliberately sacrificed the niceties of literary taste to the greater task of making Englishmen on both sides of the Atlantic real Christians. Even so, the style of some of his more literary productions is a model of lucidity and grace.

But my main point here is to echo Mr. Birrell's final statement, that " we can learn better from Wesley's ' Journal ' than from anywhere else what manner of man Wesley was, and the character of the times during which he lived and moved and had his being." My co-religionists and all who love the most characteristic qualities of modern English life are under a deep debt of obligation to my friend Mr. Parker and his publishers for giving them an opportunity of studying the eventful eighteenth century of English history at its centre and fountain-head.

The fact that this edition of the work has been condensed is no drawback. The " Journal," as originally published, was itself condensed by Wesley. The Wesleyan Book Room has in its possession large unpublished portions of the manuscript, much of which will be included in the standard edition which the Wesleyan Methodist Editor has now in hand ; but for popular purposes Mr. Parker's edition will answer all important ends, and will give Englishmen for the first time an opportunity of reading in a handy form one of the most important, instructive, and entertaining books ever published in the English language.

Of course Mr. Parker alone is responsible for the selection of the portions of the " Journal " which appear in this volume.

HUGH PRICE HUGHES.

ADELBODEN, *May* 30, 1902.

AN APPRECIATION OF
JOHN WESLEY'S JOURNAL*

BY AUGUSTINE BIRRELL, K.C.

JOHN WESLEY, born as he was in 1703 and dying as he did in 1791, covers as nearly as mortal man may, the whole of the eighteenth century, of which he was one of the most typical and certainly the most strenuous figure.

He began his published Journal on October 14, 1735, and its last entry is under date Sunday, October 24, 1790, when in the morning he explained to a numerous congregation in Spitalfields Church "The Whole Armour of God," and in the afternoon enforced to a still larger audience in St. Paul's, Shadwell, the great truth, "One thing is needful," the last words of the Journal being "I hope many even then resolved to choose the better part."

Between those two Octobers there lies the most amazing record of human exertion ever penned or endured.

I do not know whether I am likely to have among my readers any one who has ever contested an English or Scottish county in a parliamentary election since household suffrage. If I have, that tired soul will know

* Reprinted in part from *Miscellanies*, by Augustine Birrell (Elliot Stock), by permission of the author and the publishe·

how severe is the strain of its three weeks, and how impossible it seemed at the end of the first week that you should be able to keep it going for another fortnight, and how when the last night arrived you felt that had the strife been accidentally prolonged another seven days you must have perished by the wayside.

Contesting the Three Kingdoms

Well, John Wesley contested the three kingdoms in the cause of Christ during a campaign which lasted forty years.

He did it for the most part on horseback. He paid more turnpikes than any man who ever bestrode a beast. Eight thousand miles was his annual record for many a long year, during each of which he seldom preached less frequently than five thousand times. Had he but preserved his scores at all the inns where he lodged, they would have made by themselves a history of prices. And throughout it all he never knew what depression of spirits meant—though he had much to try him, suits in chancery and a jealous wife.

In the course of this unparalleled contest Wesley visited again and again the most out of the way districts —the remotest corners of England—places which to-day lie far removed even from the searcher after the picturesque.

In 1899, when the map of England looks like a gridiron of railways, none but the sturdiest of pedestrians, the most determined of cyclists can retrace the steps of Wesley and his horse, and stand by the rocks and the natural amphitheatres in Cornwall and Northumberland, in Lancashire and Berkshire, where he preached his gospel to the heathen.

Exertion so prolonged, enthusiasm so sustained, argues a remarkable man, while the organisation he created, the system he founded, the view of life he promulgated, is still a great fact among us. No other name than Wesley's lies embalmed as his does. Yet he is not a popular figure. Our standard historians have dismissed him curtly. The fact is, Wesley puts your ordinary historian out of conceit with himself.

How much easier to weave into your page the gossip of Horace Walpole, to enliven it with a heartless jest of George Selwyn's, to make it blush with sad stories of the extravagance of Fox, to embroider it with the rhetoric of Burke, to humanise it with the talk of Johnson, to discuss the rise and fall of administrations, the growth and decay of the constitution, than to follow John Wesley into the streets of Bristol, or on to the bleak moors near Burslem, when he met, face to face in all their violence, all their ignorance, and all their generosity the living men, women, and children who made up the nation.

A Book of Plots, Plays and Novels

It has perhaps also to be admitted that to found great organisations is to build your tomb—a splendid tomb, it may be, a veritable sarcophagus, but none the less a tomb. John Wesley's chapels lie a little heavily on John Wesley. Even so do the glories of Rome make us forgetful of the grave in Syria.

It has been said that Wesley's character lacks charm, that mighty antiseptic. It is not easy to define charm, which is not a catalogue of qualities, but a mixture. Let no one deny charm to Wesley who has not read his Journal. Southey's Life is a dull, almost a stupid book which happily there is no need to read. Read the Journal, which is a book full of plots and plays and novels, which quivers with life and is crammed full of character.

Wesley's Family Stock

John Wesley came of a stock which had been much harassed and put about by our unhappy religious difficulties. Politics, business, and religion are the three things Englishmen are said to worry themselves about. The Wesleys early took up with religion. John Wesley's great-grandfather and grandfather were both ejected from their livings in 1662, and the grandfather was so bullied and oppressed by the Five Mile Act that he early gave up the ghost. Whereupon his remains were refused what is called Christian burial, though a holier and more primitive man never drew breath. This poor, persecuted spirit left two sons according to the flesh, Matthew and Samuel; and Samuel it was who in his turn became the father of John and Charles Wesley.

Samuel Wesley, though minded to share the lot, hard though that lot was, of his progenitors, had the moderation of mind, the Christian conservatism which ever marked the family, and being sent to a dissenting college, became disgusted with the ferocity and bigotry he happened there to encounter. Those were the days of the Calf's Head Club and feastings on the 29th of January, graceless meals for which Samuel Wesley had no stomach. His turn was for the things that are " quiet, wise, and good." He departed from the dissenting seminary and in 1685 entered himself as a poor scholar at Exeter College, Oxford. He brought £2 6s. with him, and as for prospects, he had none. Exeter received him.

During the eighteenth century our two universities, famous despite their faults, were always open to the poor scholar who was ready to subscribe, not to boat clubs or cricket clubs, but to the Thirty-nine Articles. Three archbishops of Canterbury during the eighteenth century were the sons of small tradesmen. There was, in fact, much less snobbery and money-worship during the century when the British empire was being won than during the century when it is being talked about.

Samuel Wesley was allowed to remain at Oxford, where he supported himself by devices known to his tribe, and when he left the university to be ordained he had clear in his pouch, after discharging his few debts, £10 15s. He had thus made £8 9s. out of his university, and had his education, as it were, thrown in for nothing. He soon obtained a curacy in London and married a daughter of the well-known ejected clergyman, Dr. Annesley, about whom you may read in another eighteenth-century book "The Life and Errors of John Dunton."

Wesley's Mother

The mother of the Wesleys was a remarkable woman, though cast in a mould not much to our minds nowadays. She had nineteen children, and greatly prided herself on having taught them, one after another, by frequent chastisements to, what do you think? to cry softly. She had theories of education and strength of will, and of arm too, to carry them out.

She knew Latin and Greek, and though a stern, forbidding, almost an unfeeling, parent, she was successful in winning and retaining not only the respect but the affection of such of her huge family as lived to grow up. But out of the nineteen, thirteen early succumbed. Infant mortality was one of the great facts of the eighteenth century whose Rachels had to learn to cry softly over their dead babes. The mother of the Wesleys thought more of her children's souls than of their bodies.

A Domestic Squall

The revolution of 1688 threatened to disturb the early married life of Samuel Wesley and his spouse.

The husband wrote a pamphlet in which he defended revolution principles, but the wife secretly adhered to the old cause; nor was it until a year before Dutch William's death that the rector made the discovery that the wife of his bosom, who had sworn to obey him and regard him as her over-lord, was not in the habit of saying Amen to his fervent prayers on behalf of his suffering sovereign. An explanation was demanded and the truth extracted, namely, that in the opinion of the rector's wife her true king lived over the water. The rector at once refused to live with Mrs. Wesley any longer until she recanted. This she refused to do, and for a twelvemonth the couple dwelt apart, when William III. having the good sense to die, a reconciliation became possible. If John Wesley was occasionally a little pig-headed, need one wonder?

The story of the fire at Epworth Rectory and the miraculous escape of the infant John was once a tale as well known as Alfred in the neat-herd's hut, and pictures of it still hang up in many a collier's home.

John Wesley received a sound classical education at Charterhouse and Christ Church, and remained all his life very much the scholar and the gentleman. No company was too good for John Wesley, and nobody knew better than he did that had he cared to carry his powerful intelligence, his flawless constitution, and his infinite capacity for taking pains into any of the markets of the world, he must have earned for himself place, fame, and fortune.

Coming, however, as he did of a theological stock, having a saint for a father and a notable devout woman for a mother, Wesley from his early days learned to regard religion as the business of his life, just as the younger Pitt came to regard the House of Commons as the future theatre of his actions.

"My Jack is Fellow of Lincoln"

After a good deal of heart-searching and theological talk with his mother, Wesley was ordained a deacon by the excellent Potter, afterward Primate, but then (1725) Bishop of Oxford. In the following year Wesley was elected a Fellow of Lincoln, to the great delight of his father. "Whatever I am," said the good old man, "my Jack is Fellow of Lincoln."

.   .   .   .   .

Wesley's motive never eludes us. In his early manhood, after being greatly affected by Jeremy Taylor's "Holy Living and Dying" and the "Imitatio Christi," and by Law's "Serious Call" and "Christian Perfection," he met "a serious man" who said to him, "Sir, you wish to serve God and go to heaven. Remember you cannot serve Him alone. You must therefore find companions or make them. The Bible knows nothing of solitary religion."

He was very confident, this serious man, and Wesley never forgot his message. "You must find companions or make them. The Bible knows nothing of solitary religion." These words for ever sounded in Wesley's ears, determining his theology, which rejected the stern individualism of Calvin, and fashioning his whole polity, his famous class meetings and generally gregarious methods.

> Therefore to him it was given
> Many to save with himself.

We may continue the quotation and apply to Wesley the words of Mr. Arnold's memorial to his father:

> Languor was not in his heart,
> Weakness not in his word,
> Weariness not on his brow.

If you ask what is the impression left upon the reader of the Journal as to the condition of England question, the answer will vary very much with the tenderness of the reader's conscience and with the extent of his acquaintance with the general behaviour of mankind at all times and in all places.

No Sentimentalist

Wesley himself is no alarmist, no sentimentalist, he never gushes, seldom exaggerates, and always writes on an easy level. Naturally enough he clings to the supernatural and is always disposed to believe in the *bona fides* of ghosts and the diabolical origin of strange noises, but outside this realm of speculation, Wesley describes things as he saw them. In the first published words of his friend, Dr. Johnson, " he meets with no basilisks that destroy with their eyes, his crocodiles devour their prey without tears, and his cataracts fall from the rocks without deafening the neighbouring inhabitants."

Wesley's humour is of the species donnish, and his modes and methods quietly persistent.

Wesley's Humour

" On Thursday, May 20 (1742), I set out. The next afternoon I stopped a little at Newport-Pagnell and then rode on till I overtook a serious man with whom I immediately fell into conversation. He presently gave me to know what his opinions were, therefore I said nothing to contradict them. But that did not content him. He was quite uneasy to know ' whether I held the doctrines of the decrees as he did '; but I told him over and over ' We had better keep to practical things lest we should be angry at one another.' And so we did for two miles till he caught me unawares and dragged me into the dispute before I knew where I was. He then grew warmer and warmer; told me I was rotten at heart and supposed I was one of John Wesley's followers. I told him ' No. I am John Wesley himself.' Upon which

> *Improvisum aspris Veluti qui sentibus anguem*
> *Presset——*

he would gladly have run away outright. But being the better mounted of the two I kept close to his side and endeavoured to show him his heart till we came into the street of Northampton."

What a picture have we here of a fine May morning in 1742, the unhappy Calvinist trying to shake off the Arminian Wesley! But he cannot do it! *John Wesley is the better mounted of the two*, and so they scamper together into Northampton.

The England described in the Journal is an England still full of theology; all kinds of queer folk abound;

strange subjects are discussed in odd places. There
was drunkenness and cock-fighting, no doubt, but there
was also Deists, Mystics, Swedenborgians, Antinomians,
Necessitarians, Anabaptists, Quakers, nascent heresies,
and slow-dying delusions. Villages were divided into
rival groups, which fiercely argued the nicest points in
the aptest language. Nowadays in one's rambles a man
is as likely to encounter a grey badger as a black
Calvinist.

England in Wesley's Day

The clergy of the Established Church were jealous of
Wesley's interference in their parishes, nor was this
unnatural—he was not a Nonconformist but a brother
churchman. What right had he to be so peripatetic?
But Wesley seldom records any instance of gross clerical
misconduct. Of one drunken parson he does indeed
tell us, and he speaks disapprovingly of another whom
he found one very hot day consuming a pot of beer in a
lone ale-house. I am bound to confess I have never
had any but kindly feelings toward that thirsty eccle-
siastic. What, I wonder, was he thinking of as Wesley
rode by—*Libres Méditations d'un Solitaire Inconnu*—
unpublished !

When Wesley, with that dauntless courage of his, a
courage which never forsook him, which he wore on
every occasion with the delightful ease of a soldier,
pushed his way into fierce districts, amid rough miners
dwelling in their own village communities almost outside
the law, what most strikes one with admiration, not less
in Wesley's Journal than in George Fox's (a kindred
though earlier volume), is the essential fitness for freedom
of our rudest populations. They were coarse and brutal

and savage, but rarely did they fail to recognise the high
character and lofty motives of the dignified mortal who
had travelled so far to speak to them.

The Mobs He Met

Wesley was occasionally hustled, and once or twice
pelted with mud and stones, but at no time were his
sufferings at the hands of the mob to be compared with
the indignities it was long the fashion to heap upon the
heads of parliamentary candidates. The mob knew and
appreciated the difference between a Bubb Dodington
and a John Wesley.

I do not think any ordinary Englishman will be much
horrified at the demeanour of the populace. If there
was disturbance it was usually quelled. At Norwich two
soldiers who disturbed a congregation were seized and
carried before their commanding officer, who ordered
them to be soundly whipped. In Wesley's opinion they
richly deserved all they got. He was no sentimentalist,
although an enthusiast.

Where the reader of the Journal will be shocked is
when his attention is called to the public side of the
country—to the state of the gaols—to Newgate, to
Bethlehem, to the criminal code—to the brutality of so
many of the judges, and the harshness of the magistrates,
to the supineness of the bishops, to the extinction in
high places of the missionary spirit—in short, to the
heavy slumber of humanity.

Wesley was full of compassion, of a compassion wholly
free from hysterics and like exaltative. In public affairs
his was the composed zeal of a Howard. His efforts to
penetrate the dark places were long in vain. He says in
his dry way: " They won't let me go to Bedlam because

they say I make the inmates mad, or into Newgate because I make them wicked." The reader of the Journal will be at no loss to see what these sapient magistrates meant.

Wesley was a terribly exciting preacher, quiet though his manner was. He pushed matters home without flinching. He made people cry out and fall down, nor did it surprise him, that they should.

* * * * *

Ever a Preacher

If you want to get into the last century, to feel its pulses throb beneath your finger, be content sometimes to leave the letters of Horace Walpole unturned, resist the drowsy temptation to waste your time over the learned triflers who sleep in the seventeen volumes of Nichols, nay even deny yourself your annual reading of Boswell or your biennial retreat with Sterne, and ride up and down the country with the greatest force of the eighteenth century in England.

No man lived nearer the centre than John Wesley. Neither Clive nor Pitt, neither Mansfield nor Johnson. You cannot cut him out of our national life. No single figure influenced so many minds, no single voice touched so many hearts. No other man did such a life's work for England.

As a writer he has not achieved distinction, he was no Athanasius, no Augustine, he was ever a preacher and an organiser, a labourer in the service of humanity ; but happily for us his Journals remain, and from them we can learn better than from anywhere else what manner of man he was, and the character of the times during which he lived and moved and had his being.

AUGUSTINE BIRRELL.

WESLEY'S LAST HOURS

BY ONE WHO WAS PRESENT *

On Thursday [February 24th, 1791] Mr. Wesley paid his last visit to that lovely place and family, Mr. Wolff's, at Balaam, which I have often heard him speak of with pleasure and much affection. Here Mr. Rogers said he was cheerful, and seemed nearly as well as usual, till Friday, about breakfast time, when he seemed very heavy.

About eleven o'clock Mrs. Wolff brought him home : I was struck with his manner of getting out of the coach, and going into the house, but more so as he went upstairs, and when he sat down in the chair. I ran for some refreshment, but before I could get anything for him he had sent Mr. R—— out of the room, and desired not to be interrupted for half-an-hour by any one, adding, not even if Joseph Bradford come.

Mr. Bradford came a few minutes after, and as soon as the limited time was expired, went into the room ; immediately after he came out and desired me to mull some wine with spices and carry it to Mr. Wesley : he

* This account (condensed) was written by Betsy Ritchie, one of the saints of early Methodism.   At the time she was about thirty-nine, and for the last two months of Wesley's life was his constant companion.

drank a little and seemed sleepy. In a few minutes he was seized with sickness, threw it up, and said, " I must lie down." We immediately sent for Dr. Whitehead : on his coming in Mr. Wesley smiled and said, " Doctor, they are more afraid than hurt." He lay most of the day, with a quick pulse, burning fever and extremely sleepy.

Saturday the 26th, he continued much the same; spoke but little, and if roused to answer a question, or take a little refreshment (which was seldom more than a spoonful at a time) soon dozed again.

On Sunday morning, with a little of Mr. Bradford's help, Mr. Wesley got up, took a cup of tea, and seemed much better. Many of our friends were all hopes : yet Dr. Whitehead said, he was not out of danger from his present complaints.

Monday the 28th, his weakness increased apace and his friends in general being greatly alarmed, Dr. Whitehead was desirous they should call in another physician. Mr. Bradford mentioned his desire to our Honoured Father, which he absolutely refused, saying, " Dr. Whitehead knows my condition better than any one; I am perfectly satisfied and will not have any one else." He slept most of the day, spoke but little; yet that little testified how much his whole heart was taken up in the case of the Churches, the glory of God, and the things pertaining to that kingdom to which he was hastening. Once in a low, but very distinct manner, he said, " There is no way into the holiest but by the blood of Jesus." Had he had strength at the time, it seemed as if he would have said more.

Tuesday, March 1st, after a very restless night (though, when asked whether he was in pain, he generally answered " No," and never complained through his whole illness, except once, when he said that he felt a pain in his left breast, when he drew his breath), he began singing:

> "All glory to God in the sky,
> And peace upon earth be restor'd."

[Having sung two verses] his strength failed, but after lying still awhile he called on Mr. Bradford to give him a pen and ink; he brought them, but the right hand had well-nigh forgot its cunning, and those active fingers which had been the blessed instruments of spiritual consolation and pleasing instruction to thousands, could no longer perform their office. Some time after, he said to me, "I want to write": I brought him a pen and ink, and on putting the pen into his hand, and holding the paper before him, he said, "I cannot." I replied, "Let me write for you, sir; tell me what you would say." "Nothing," returned he, "but that God is with us." In the forenoon he said, "I will get up." While his things were getting ready, he broke out in a manner which, considering his extreme weakness, astonished us all, in these blessed words:

> "I'll praise my Maker while I've breath,
> And when my voice is lost in death,
>   Praise shall employ my nobler pow'rs;
> My days of praise shall ne'er be past,
> While life, and thought, and being last,
>   Or immortality endures."

Which were also the last words our Reverend and dear Father ever gave out in the City Road Chapel, viz., on Tuesday evening before preaching from, "We through the Spirit wait," &c.

When he got into his chair, we saw him change for death: but he, regardless of his dying frame, said, with

a weak voice, " Lord, Thou givest strength to those that
can speak, and to those that cannot : Speak, Lord, to all
our hearts, and let them know that Thou loosest tongues."
He then sang :

> " To Father, Son, and Holy Ghost,
> Who sweetly all agree."

Here his voice failed him, and after gasping for breath,
he said, " Now we have done—Let us all go." We were
obliged to lay him down on the bed from which he rose
no more : but after lying still, and sleeping a little, he
called me to him and said, " Betsy, you Mr. Bradford, &c.,
pray and praise." We knelt down, and truly our hearts
were filled with the divine presence ; the room seemed
to be filled with God.

A little after he spoke to Mr. Bradford about the key
and contents of his bureau ; while he attended to the
directions given him, Mr. Wesley called me and said, "I
would have all things ready for my Executors, Mr. Wolff,
Mr. Horton, and Mr. Marriott "—here his voice again
failed ; but taking breath he added, " Let me be buried
in nothing but what is woollen, and let my corpse be
carried in my coffin into the Chapel." Then, as if done
with all below, he again begged we would pray and praise.

The next pleasing awful scene was the great exertion
he made in order to make Mr. B. (who had not left the
room) understand that he fervently desired a sermon he
had written on the Love of God should be scattered
abroad, and given away to everybody. Something else
he wished to say, but, alas ! his speech failed ; and those
lips which used to feed many were no longer able (except
when particular strength was given) to convey their accustomed sounds.

A little after, Mr. Horton coming in, we hoped that if he had anything of moment on his mind, which he wished to communicate, he would again try to tell us what it was, and that either Mr. Horton, or some of those who were most used to hear our dear Father's dying voice would be able to interpret his meaning; but though he strove to speak, we were still unsuccessful: finding we could not understand what he said, he paused a little, and then with all the remaining strength he had, cried out, "The best of all is, God is with us";—and then, as if to assert the faithfulness of our promise-keeping Jehovah, and comfort the hearts of his weeping friends, lifting up his dying arm in token of victory, and raising his feeble voice with a holy triumph not to be expressed, again repeated the heart-reviving words, "The best of all is, God is with us!"

Some time after, giving him something to wet his parched lips, he said, "It will not do, we must take the consequence; never mind the poor carcase." Pausing a little, he cried, "The clouds drop fatness!" and soon after, "The Lord is with us, the God of Jacob is our refuge!" He then called us to prayer. Mr. Broadbent was again the mouth of our full hearts, and though Mr Wesley was greatly exhausted by these exertions, he appeared still more fervent in spirit. Most of the night following, though he was often heard attempting to repeat the psalm before-mentioned, he could only get out,

" I'll praise —— I'll praise —— ! "

On Wednesday morning we found the closing scene drew near. Mr. Bradford, his faithful friend, and most affectionate son, prayed with him, and the last word he was heard to articulate was, "Farewell!" A few minutes

before ten, while Miss Wesley, Mr. Horton, Mr. Bracken-
bury, Mr. and Mrs. Rogers, Dr. Whitehead, Mr. Broadbent, Mr. Whitfield, Mr, Bradford, and E. R. were
kneeling around his bed ; according to his often expressed
desire, without a lingering groan, this man of God
gathered up his feet in the presence of his brethren !

IMPORTANT WESLEY DATES

Wesley Born . . . . June 17, 1703
Epworth Parsonage Burned 1709
Goes to Charterhouse School 1714
Enters Christ Church, Oxford 1720
Ordained Deacon 1725
Wesley's First Sermon, Preached at S. Leigh . . 1725
Elected Fellow of Lincoln College 1726
Left Oxford to Assist his Father 1727
Holy Club Started 1727
Ordained Priest 1728
Returned to Oxford as Tutor 1729
Went to Georgia 1735
Published "Journal" Begins . . . . Oct. 14, 1735
Returned to England 1738
Met Peter Böhler . . . . . . Feb. 7, 1738
Famous Meeting in Aldersgate Street when Wesley's
  "heart was strangely warmed" . . May 24, 1738
Wesley Begins Open Air Preaching 1739
Foundery (the Cradle of Methodism) Taken . . 1739
First Methodist Preaching-place Built at Bristol . . 1739
Lay Preachers Employed 1741
Methodist Classes Established at Bristol . . . 1742
First Conference (London) 1744
Wesley Married 1751
City Road Chapel Built 1778

Wesley's Wife Died 1781
Wesley's Last Field Preaching (at Winchelsea) Oct. 6, 1790
Last Entry in his Journal . . . . Oct. 24, 1790
Last Sermon in City Road . . . . Feb. 22, 1791
His Last Sermon (Leatherhead) . . . Feb. 23, 1791
His Last Letter (to Wilberforce) . . . Feb. 24, 1791
Returned to City Road House to Die . . Feb. 25, 1791
Wesley Died in his Eighty-eighth Year . . March 2, 1791

PROGRESS OF METHODISM

When Wesley died in 1791, there were in England about 79,000 Methodists, Members of Society Classes, and 312 Ministers in Circuits. In America and Canada there were about 40,000 or 50,000 Methodists. Total 119,000.

At the Œcumenical Methodist Conference held in London in 1901, the marvellous growth of Methodism— the result of Wesley's work—was shown in the following figures ; they indicate the extent of Methodism throughout the world : Ministers, 48,334 ; Local Preachers, 104,786 ; Churches, 89,087 ; Members, 7,659,285 ; Sunday Schools, 81,228 : Teachers and Officers, 861,392 ; Scholars 7,077,079 ; and Adherents, 24,899,421.

WESLEY'S JOURNAL

THE first entry in Wesley's Journal is that of October 14, 1735. But the following letter, which Wesley published with the first edition of his Journal, precedes it, as it describes the incidents which led to the formation of the Holy Club and to the social activities from which, as the Journal shows, Methodism has evolved.

The letter was written from Oxford in 1732 to Mr. Morgan, whose son is mentioned. It runs thus:

Wesley Begins his Work

In November 1729, at which time I came to reside at Oxford, your son [Mr. Morgan], my brother, myself, and one more, agreed to spend three or four evenings in a week together. Our design was to read over the classics, which we had before read in private, on common nights, and on Sunday some book in divinity. In the summer following, Mr. M. told me he had called at the gaol, to see a man who was condemned for killing his wife; and that, from the talk he had with one of the debtors, he verily believed it would do much good, if any one would be at the pains of now and then speaking with them.

This he so frequently repeated, that on August 24, 1730, my brother and I walked with him to the castle. We were so well satisfied with our conversation there,

A

that we agreed to go thither once or twice a week;
which we had not done long, before he desired me to
go with him to see a poor woman in the town, who was
sick.   In this employment too, when we came to reflect
upon it, we believed it would be worth while to spend
an hour or two in a week; provided the minister of the
parish, in which any such person was, were not against
it.   But that we might not depend wholly on our own
judgments, I wrote an account to my father of our
whole design; withal begging that he, who had lived
seventy years in the world, and seen as much of it as
most private men have ever done, would advise us
whether we had yet gone too far, and whether we
should now stand still, or go forward.

Origin of the Holy Club

In pursuance of [his] directions, I immediately went to
Mr. Gerard, the Bishop of Oxford's chaplain, who was
likewise the person that took care of the prisoners when
any were condemned to die (at other times they were
left to their own care): I proposed to him our design of
serving them as far as we could, and my own intention
to preach there once a month, if the bishop approved
of it.   He much commended our design, and said he
would answer for the bishop's approbation, to whom he
would take the first opportunity of mentioning it.   It
was not long before he informed me he had done so,
and that his lordship not only gave his permission, but
was greatly pleased with the undertaking, and hoped it
would have the desired success.

Soon after, a gentleman of Merton College, who was
one of our little company, which now consisted of five
persons, acquainted us that he had been much rallied
the day before for being a member of the Holy Club;

and that it was become a common topic of mirth at his college, where they had found out several of our customs, to which we were ourselves utter strangers. Upon this I consulted my father again.

. . . .

Upon [his] encouragement we still continued to meet together as usual; and to confirm one another, as well as we could, in our resolutions, to communicate as often as we had opportunity (which is here once a week); and do what service we could to our acquaintance, the prisoners, and two or three poor families in the town.

Wesley Sails for America

1735. Tuesday, October 14.—Mr. Benjamin Ingham, of Queen's College, Oxford; Mr. Charles Delamotte, son of a merchant, in London, who had offered himself some days before; my brother, Charles Wesley, and myself, took boat for Gravesend, in order to embark for Georgia.

Our end in leaving our native country was not to avoid want (God having given us plenty of temporal blessings), nor to gain the dung or dross of riches or honour; but singly this—to save our souls; to live wholly to the glory of God. In the afternoon we found the "Simmonds" off Gravesend, and immediately went on board.

Fri. 17.—I began to learn German, in order to converse with the Germans, six-and-twenty of whom we had on board. On Sunday, the weather being fair and calm, we had the morning service on quarter-deck. I now first preached extempore, and then administered the Lord's supper to six or seven communicants.

Mon. 20.—Believing the denying ourselves, even in the smallest instances, might, by the blessing of God, be helpful to us, we wholly left off the use of flesh and wine, and confined ourselves to vegetable food—chiefly rice and biscuit.

Tues. 21.—We sailed from Gravesend. When we were past about half the Goodwin Sands, the wind suddenly failed. Had the calm continued till ebb, the ship had probably been lost. But the gale sprung up again in an hour, and carried us into the Downs.

We now began to be a little regular. Our common way of living was this: From four in the morning till five each of us used private prayer. From five to seven we read the Bible together, carefully comparing it (that we might not lean to our own understandings) with the writings of the earliest ages. At seven we breakfasted. At eight were the public prayers. From nine to twelve I usually learned German, and Mr. Delamotte, Greek. My brother writ sermons, and Mr. Ingham instructed the children. At twelve we met to give an account to one another what we had done since our last meeting, and what we designed to do before our next. About one we dined.

Life on Board

The time from dinner to four we spent in reading to those whom each of us had taken in charge, or in speaking to them severally, as need required. At four were the evening prayers; when either the second lesson was explained (as it always was in the morning), or the children were catechised and instructed before the congregation. From five to six we again used private prayer. From six to seven I read in our cabin to two or three of the passengers (of whom there were about eighty English on board), and each of my brethren to a few more in theirs.

At seven I joined with the Germans in their public service, while Mr. Ingham was reading between the decks to as many as desired to hear. At eight we met again to exhort and instruct one another. Between nine and ten we went to bed, where neither the roaring of the sea nor the motion of the ship could take away the refreshing sleep which God gave us.

Fri. 31.—We sailed out of the Downs. At eleven at night I was waked by a great noise. I soon found there was no danger. But the bare apprehension of it gave me a lively conviction what manner of men those ought to be who are every moment on the brink of eternity.

Sat. Nov. 1.—We came to St. Helen's harbour, and the next day into Cowes road. The wind was fair, but we waited for the man-of-war which was to sail with us. This was a happy opportunity of instructing our fellow travellers.

Sun. 23.—At night I was awaked by the tossing of the ship and roaring of the wind, and plainly showed I was unfit, for I was unwilling, to die.

Wed. Dec. 10.—We sailed from Cowes, and in the afternoon passed the Needles. Here the ragged rocks, with the waves dashing and foaming at the foot of them, and the white side of the island rising to such a height, perpendicular from the beach, gave a strong idea of " Him that spanneth the heavens, and holdeth the waters in the hollow of His hand !"

1736. Thur. Jan. 15.—Complaint being made to Mr. Oglethorpe, of the unequal distribution of the water among the passengers, he appointed new officers to take charge of it. At this the old ones and their friends were highly exasperated against us, to whom they imputed the change.

Sat. 17.—Many people were very impatient at the contrary wind. At seven in the evening they were quieted by a storm. It rose higher and higher till nine. About nine the sea broke over us from stem to stern; burst through the windows of the state cabin, where three or four of us were, and covered us all over, though a bureau sheltered me from the main shock. About eleven I lay down in the great cabin, and in a short time fell asleep, though very uncertain whether I should wake alive, and much ashamed of my unwillingness to die. O how pure in heart must he be, who would rejoice to appear before God at a moment's warning! Toward morning, " He rebuked the winds and the sea, and there was a great calm."

Memorable Atlantic Storms

Fri. 23.—In the evening another storm began. In the morning it increased, so that they were forced to let the ship drive. I could not but say to myself, " How is it that thou hast no faith ? " being still unwilling to die. About one in the afternoon, almost as soon as I had stepped out of the great cabin-door, the sea did not break as usual, but came with a full, smooth tide over the side of the ship. I was vaulted over with water in a moment, and so stunned that I scarce expected to lift up my head again, till the sea should give up her dead. But thanks be to God, I received no hurt at all. About midnight the storm ceased.

Sun. 25.—At noon our third storm began. At four it was more violent than before. At seven I went to the Germans. I had long before observed the great seriousness of their behaviour. Of their humility they had given a continual proof, by performing those servile offices for the other passengers, which none of the

English would undertake; for which they desired, and would receive no pay, saying, "it was good for their proud hearts," and "their loving Saviour had done more for them." And every day had given them an occasion of showing a meekness, which no injury could move. If they were pushed, struck, or thrown down, they rose again and went away; but no complaint was found in their mouth. There was now an opportunity of trying whether they were delivered from the spirit of fear, as well as from that of pride, anger and revenge.

In the midst of the psalm wherewith their service began, the sea broke over, split the mainsail in pieces, covered the ship, and poured in between the decks, as if the great deep had already swallowed us up. A terrible screaming began among the English. The Germans calmly sung on. I asked one of them afterwards, "Was you not afraid?" He answered, "I thank God, no." I asked, "But were not your women and children afraid?" He replied, mildly, "No; our women and children are not afraid to die."

Fri. 30.—We had another storm, which did us no other harm than splitting the fore-sail. Our bed being wet, I laid me down on the floor, and slept sound till morning. And, I believe, I shall not find it needful to go to bed (as it is called) any more.

Sun. Feb. 1.—We spoke with a ship of Carolina; and Wednesday, 4, came within soundings. About noon, the trees were visible from the masts, and in the afternoon from the main deck. In the evening lesson were these words: "A great door, and effectual, is opened." O let no one shut it!

Thur. 5.—Between two and three in the afternoon, God brought us all safe into the Savannah river. We cast anchor near Tybee Island, where the groves of pines, running along the shore, made an agreeable prospect, showing, as it were, the bloom of spring in the depth of winter.

Wesley Arrives in Georgia

Fri. 6.—About eight in the morning, we first set foot on American ground. It was a small uninhabited island, over against Tybee. Mr. Oglethorpe led us to a rising ground, where we all kneeled down to give thanks. He then took boat for Savannah. When the rest of the people were come on shore, we called our little flock together to prayers.

Sat. 7.—Mr. Oglethorpe returned from Savannah with Mr. Spangenberg, one of the pastors of the Germans. I soon found what spirit he was of; and asked his advice with regard to my own conduct. He said, "My brother, I must first ask you one or two questions. Have you the witness within yourself? Does the Spirit of God bear witness with your spirit, that you are a child of God?" I was surprised, and knew not what to answer. He observed it, and asked, "Do you know Jesus Christ?" I paused, and said, "I know he is the Saviour of the world." "True," replied he; "but do you know he has saved you?" I answered, "I hope he has died to save me." He only added, "Do you know yourself?" I said, "I do." But I fear they were vain words.

Sat. 14.—About one, Tomo Chachi, his nephew Thleeanouhee, his wife Sinauky, with two more women, and two or three Indian children, came on board. As soon as we came in, they all rose and shook us by the hand; and Tomo Chachi (one Mr. Musgrove interpreted) spoke as follows:

"I am glad you are come. When I was in England, I desired that some would speak the great word to me and my nation then desired to hear it; but now we are all in confusion. Yet I am glad you are come. I will go up and speak to the wise men of our nation; and I hope they will hear. But we would not be made Christians as the Spaniards make Christians: we would be taught, before we are baptized."

I answered, "There is but One, He that sitteth in heaven, who is able to teach man wisdom. Though we are come so far, we know not whether He will please to teach you by us or no. If He teaches you, you will learn wisdom, but we can do nothing." We then withdrew.

Thur. 19.—My brother and I took boat, and, passing by Savannah, went to pay our first visit in America to the poor heathens.

Begins his Ministry at Savannah

Sun. March 7.—I entered upon my ministry at Savannah, by preaching on the epistle for the day, being the thirteenth of the first of Corinthians. In the second lesson (Luke xviii.) was our Lord's prediction of the treatment which he himself (and, consequently, his followers) was to meet with from the world. "Verily I say unto you, There is no man that hath left house, or friends, or brethren, or wife, or children, for the kingdom of God's sake, who shall not receive manifold more in this present time, and in the world to come life everlasting."

Yet, notwithstanding these declarations of our Lord—notwithstanding my own repeated experience—notwithstanding the experience of all the sincere followers of Christ whom I have ever talked with, read or heard of; nay, and the reason of the thing evincing to a demonstration that all who love not the light must hate Him who is continually labouring to pour it in upon them;

I do here bear witness against myself, that when I saw the number of people crowding into the church, the deep attention with which they received the word, and the seriousness that afterwards sat on all their faces; I could scarce refrain from giving the lie to experience and reason and Scripture all together.

I could hardly believe that the greater, the far greater part of this attentive, serious people would hereafter trample under foot that word, and say all manner of evil falsely of him that spake it.

Mon. 15.—Mr. Quincy going for Carolina, I removed into the minister's house. It is large enough for a larger family than ours, and has many conveniences, besides a good garden.

Tues. 30.—Mr. Ingham, coming from Frederica, brought me letters, pressing me to go thither. The next day Mr. Delamotte and I began to try, whether life might not as well be sustained by one sort as by variety of food. We chose to make the experiment with bread; and were never more vigorous and healthy than while we tasted nothing else.

"I Waked under Water"

Sun. April 4.—About four in the afternoon I set out for Frederica, in a pettiawga—a sort of flat-bottomed barge. The next evening we anchored near Skidoway Island, where the water, at flood, was twelve or fourteen foot deep. I wrapped myself up from head to foot, in a large cloak, to keep off the sand flies, and lay down on the quarter-deck. Between one and two I waked under water, being so fast asleep that I did not find where I was till my mouth was full of it. Having left my cloak, I know not how, upon deck, I swam round to the other side of the pettiawga, where a boat was tied,

and climbed up by the rope without any hurt, more
than wetting my clothes.

Sat. 17.—Not finding, as yet, any door open for the
pursuing our main design, we considered in what manner
we might be most useful to the little flock at Savannah.
And we agreed: 1. To advise the more serious among
them to form themselves into a sort of little society, and
to meet once or twice a week, in order to reprove,
instruct, and exhort one another. 2. To select out of
these a smaller number for a more intimate union with
each other, which might be forwarded, partly by our
conversing singly with each, and partly by inviting them
all together to our house; and this, accordingly, we
determined to do every Sunday in the afternoon.

Mon. May 10.—I began visiting my parishioners in
order, from house to house; for which I set apart (the
time when they cannot work, because of the heat, viz.)
from twelve till three in the afternoon.

Thur. June 17.—An officer of a man-of-war, walking
just behind us, with two or three of his acquaintance,
cursed and swore exceedingly; but upon my reproving
him, seemed much moved, and gave me many thanks.

Tues. 22.—Observing much coldness in M. ——'s
behaviour, I asked him the reason of it. He answered,
"I like nothing you do. All your sermons are satires
upon particular persons, therefore I will never hear you
more; and all the people are of my mind, for we won't
hear ourselves abused.

"Beside, they say, they are Protestants. But as for
you, they cannot tell what religion you are of. They
never heard of such a religion before. They do not
know what to make of it. And then your private
behaviour: all the quarrels that have been here since
you came, have been 'long of you. Indeed there is

neither man nor woman in the town, who minds a word
you say. And so you may preach long enough; but
nobody will come to hear you."

He was too warm for hearing an answer. So I had
nothing to do but to thank him for his openness, and
walk away.

Talks to the Indians

Wed. 30.—I hoped a door was opened for going
up immediately to the Choctaws, the least polished,
that is, the least corrupted, of all the Indian nations.
But upon my informing Mr. Oglethorpe of our design,
he objected, not only the danger of being intercepted or
killed by the French there; but much more, the
inexpediency of leaving Savannah destitute of a minister.
These objections I related to our brethren in the
evening, who were all of opinion, "We ought not to go
yet."

Thur. July 1.—The Indians had an audience; and
another on Saturday, when Chicali, their head-man,
dined with Mr. Oglethorpe. After dinner, I asked the
grey-headed old man, what he thought he was made for.
He said, " He that is above knows what he made us for.
We know nothing. We are in the dark. But white
men know much. And yet white men build great
houses, as if they were to live for ever. But white men
cannot live for ever. In a little time, white men will
be dust as well as I." I told him, " If red men will
learn the good book, they may know as much as white
men. But neither we nor you can understand that
book, unless we are taught by Him that is above: and
He will not teach, unless you avoid what you already
know is not good." He answered, "I believe that.
He will not teach us while our hearts are not white.
And our men do what they know is not good: they kill

their own children. And our women do what they know is not good: they kill the child before it is born. Therefore He that is above does not send us the good book."

Mon. 26.—My brother and I set out for Charlestown, in order to his embarking for England; but the wind being contrary, we did not reach Port-Royal, forty miles from Savannah, till Wednesday evening. The next morning we left it. But the wind was so high in the afternoon, as we were crossing the neck of St. Helena's sound, that our oldest sailor cried out, " Now every one must take care for himself." I told him, " God would take care for us all." Almost as soon as the words were spoken, the mast fell. I kept on the edge of the boat, to be clear of her when she sunk (which we expected every moment), though with little prospect of swimming ashore, against such a wind and sea. But " how is it that thou hadst no faith ? " The moment the mast fell, two men caught it, and pulled it into the boat; the other three rowed with all their might, and " God gave command to the wind and seas "; so that in an hour we were safe on land.

Fearless of Rains and Dews

Mon. Aug. 2.—I set out for the Lieutenant-Governor's seat, about thirty miles from Charlestown, to deliver Mr. Oglethorpe's letters. It stands very pleasantly, on a little hill, with a vale on either side, in one of which is a thick wood; the other is planted with rice and Indian corn. I designed to have gone back by Mr. Skeen's, who has about fifty Christian negroes. But my horse tiring, I was obliged to return the straight way to Charlestown.

I had sent the boat we came in back to Savannah,

expecting a passage thither myself in Colonel Bull's. His
not going so soon, I went to Ashley-Ferry on Thursday,
intending to walk to Port-Royal. But Mr. Belinger not
only provided me a horse, but rode with me himself ten
miles, and sent his son with me to Cumbee-Ferry,
twenty miles farther; whence, having hired horses and
a guide, I came to Beaufort (or Port Royal) the next
evening. We took boat in the morning; but, the wind
being contrary, and very high, did not reach Savannah
till Sunday, in the afternoon.

Finding Mr. Oglethorpe was gone, I stayed only a
day at Savannah; and leaving Mr. Ingham and Delamotte there, set out on Tuesday morning for Frederica.
In walking to Thunderbolt I was in so heavy a shower,
that all my clothes were as wet as if I had gone through
the river. On which occasion I cannot but observe
that vulgar error, concerning the hurtfulness of the
rains and dews of America. I have been thoroughly
wet with these rains more than once; yet without any
harm at all. And I have lain many nights in the open
air, and received all the dews that fell; and so, I believe, might any one, if his constitution was not im-
paired by the softness of a genteel education.

Desires to Go Among the Indians

Tues. Nov. 23.—Mr. Oglethorpe sailed for England,
leaving Mr. Ingham, Mr. Delamotte, and me, at Savannah; but with less prospect of preaching to the Indians
than we had the first day we set foot in America.
Whenever I mentioned it, it was immediately replied,
" You cannot leave Savannah without a minister."

To this indeed my plain answer was, " I know not
that I am under any obligation to the contrary. I never
promised to stay here one month. I openly declared

both before, at, and ever since my coming hither, that I neither would nor could take charge of the English any longer than till I could go among the Indians." If it was said, "But did not the trustees of Georgia appoint you to be minister of Savannah?" I replied, "They did; but it was not done by my solicitation: it was done without either my desire or knowledge. Therefore I cannot conceive that appointment to lay me under any obligation of continuing there any longer than till a door is opened to the heathens; and this I expressly declared at the time I consented to accept of that appointment."

But though I had no other obligation not to leave Savannah now, yet that of love I could not break through: I could not resist the importunate request of the more serious parishioners, "to watch over their souls yet a little longer, till some one came who might supply my place." And this I the more willingly did, because the time was not come to preach the Gospel of peace to the heathens; all their nations being in a ferment; and Paustoobee and Mingo Mattaw having told me, in terms, in my own house, "Now our enemies are all about us, and we can do nothing but fight; but if the beloved ones should ever give us to be at peace, then we would hear the great word."

Wed. Dec. 23.—Mr. Delamotte and I, with a guide, set out to walk to the Cowpen. When we had walked two or three hours, our guide told us plainly, he did not know where we were. However, believing it could not be far off, we thought it best to go on. In an hour or two we came to a cypress-swamp, which lay directly across our way: there was not time to walk back to Savannah before night; so we walked through it, the water being about breast high.

By the time we had gone a mile beyond it, we were
out of all path; and it being now past sunset, we sat
down, intending to make a fire, and to stay there till
morning; but finding our tinder wet, we were at a stand.
I advised to walk on still; but my companions, being
faint and weary, were for lying down, which we accordingly did about six o'clock; the ground was as wet as
our clothes, which, it being a sharp frost, were soon
froze together; however, I slept till six in the morning.
There fell a heavy dew in the night, which covered us
over as white as snow. Within an hour after sunrise,
we came to a plantation; and in the evening, without
any hurt, to Savannah.

Begins to Learn Spanish

1737. Fri. March 4.—I writ the trustees for Georgia
an account of our year's expense, from March 1, 1736, to
March 1, 1737; which, deducting extraordinary expenses,
such as repairing the parsonage house, and journeys to
Frederica, amounted, for Mr. Delamotte and me, to
£44 4s. 4d.

Mon. April 4.—I began learning Spanish, in order to
converse with my Jewish parishioners; some of whom
seem nearer the mind that was in Christ than many of
those who call him Lord.

Tues. 12.—Being determined, if possible, to put a
stop to the proceedings of one in Carolina, who had
married several of my parishioners without either banns
or licence, and declared he would do so still, I set out
in a sloop for Charlestown. I landed there on Thursday,
and related the case to Mr. Garden, the Bishop of London's
Commissary, who assured me, he would take care no
such irregularity should be committed for the future.

Sun. July 3.—Immediately after the holy communion,

I mentioned to Mrs. Williamson (Mr. Causton's niece) some things which I thought reprovable in her behaviour. At this she appeared extremely angry; said she did not expect such usage from me; and at the turn of the street, through which we were walking home, went abruptly away. The next day Mrs. Causton endeavoured to excuse her; told me she was exceedingly grieved for what had passed the day before, and desired me to tell her in writing what I disliked; which I accordingly did the day following.

But first I sent Mr. Causton the following note:

" Sir,

    " To this hour you have shown yourself my friend; I ever have and ever shall acknowledge it. And it is my earnest desire that He who hath hitherto given me this blessing, would continue it still.

    " But this cannot be, unless you will allow me one request, which is not so easy an one as it appears: do not condemn me for doing, in the execution of my office, what I think it my duty to do.

    " If you can prevail upon yourself to allow me this, even when I act without respect of persons, I am persuaded there will never be, at least not long, any misunderstanding between us. For even those who seek it shall, I trust, find no occasion against me, ' except it be concerning the law of my God.'

                                        " I am, &c.

    " July 5, 1737."

Wed. 6.—Mr. Causton came to my house with Mr. Bailiff Parker and Mr. Recorder, and warmly asked, " How could you possibly think I should condemn you for executing any part of your office?" I said short, " Sir, what if I should think it the duty of my office to

B

repel one of your family from the holy communion?"
He replied, "If you repel me or my wife, I shall require
a legal reason. But I shall trouble myself about none
else. Let them look to themselves."

Warrant for Wesley's Arrest

Sun. Aug. 7.—I repelled Mrs. Williamson from the
holy communion. And Monday, 8, Mr. Recorder, of
Savannah, issued out the warrant following:

"Georgia.   Savannah ss.

"*To all Constables, Tithingmen, and others, whom these
may concern:*

"You, and each of you, are hereby required to take
the body of John Wesley, Clerk:

"And bring him before one of the Bailiffs of the said
town to answer the complaint of William Williamson and
Sophia, his wife, for defaming the said Sophia, and refusing to administer to her the sacrament of the Lord's
supper in a public congregation without cause; by
which the said William Williamson is damaged one
thousand pound sterling; and for so doing, this is your
warrant, certifying what you are to do in the premises.
Given under my hand and seal the 8th day of August,
Anno. Dom. 1737.   Tho. Christie."

Tues. 9.—Mr. Jones, the constable, served the
warrant, and carried me before Mr. Bailiff Parker and
Mr. Recorder. My answer to them was, that the giving
or refusing the Lord's supper being a matter purely
ecclesiastical, I could not acknowledge their power to
interrogate me upon it. Mr. Parker told me: "However, you must appear at the next Court, holden for
Savannah."   Mr. Williamson, who stood by, said:
"Gentlemen, I desire Mr. Wesley may give bail for his

appearance." But Mr. Parker immediately replied : " Sir, Mr. Wesley's word is sufficient."

Thur. 11.—Mr. Causton came to my house, and, among many other sharp words, said : " Make an end of this matter ; thou hadst best. My niece to be used thus ! I have drawn the sword, and I will never sheath it till I have satisfaction."

Soon after, he added : " Give the reasons of your repelling her before the whole congregation." I answered : " Sir, if you insist upon it, I will ; and so you may be pleased to tell her." He said, " Write to her, and tell her so yourself." I said. " I will " ; and after he went I wrote as follows :

" To Mrs. Sophia Williamson.

" AT Mr. Causton's request, I write once more. The rules whereby I proceed are these :

" ' So many as intend to be partakers of the holy communion, shall signify their names to the curate, at least some time the day before.' This you did not do.

" ' And if any of these have done any wrong to his neighbours, by word or deed, so that the congregation be thereby offended, the curate shall advertise him that in any wise he presume not to come to the Lord's table until he hath openly declared himself to have truly repented.'

" If you offer yourself at the Lord's table on Sunday, I will advertise you (as I have done more than once) wherein you have done wrong. And when you have openly declared yourself to have truly repented, I will administer to you the mysteries of God.

" JOHN WESLEY.

" August 11, 1737."

Mr. Delamotte carrying this, Mr. Causton said, among many other warm sayings : " I am the person that am

injured. The affront is offered to me; and I will
espouse the cause of my niece. I am ill-used, and I
will have satisfaction, if it be to be had in the world."

Which way this satisfaction was to be had, I did not
yet conceive; but on Friday and Saturday it began to
appear: Mr. Causton declared to many persons that
" Mr. Wesley had repelled Sophy from the holy communion purely out of revenge, because he had made
proposals of marriage to her which she rejected, and
married Mr. Williamson."

The Jury's Charge against Wesley

Tues. 16.—Mrs. Williamson swore to and signed an
affidavit insinuating much more than it asserted; but
asserting that Mr. Wesley had many times proposed
marriage to her, all which proposals she had rejected.
Of this I desired a copy. Mr. Causton replied: " Sir,
you may have one from any of the newspapers in
America."

On Thursday and Friday was delivered out a list of
twenty-six men, who were to meet as a grand jury on
Monday, the 22nd. But this list was called in the
next day, and twenty-four names added to it. Of this
grand jury (forty-four of whom only met), one was a
Frenchman, who did not understand English; one a
Papist, one a professed infidel, three Baptists, sixteen
or seventeen others Dissenters, and several others who
had personal quarrels against me, and had openly vowed
revenge.

To this grand jury, on Monday, the 22nd, Mr. Causton
gave a long and earnest charge, " to beware of spiritual
tyranny, and to oppose the new, illegal authority
which was usurped over their consciences." Then
Mrs. Williamson's affidavit was read; after which,

Mr. Causton delivered to the grand jury a paper, entitled :

"A list of grievances, presented by the grand jury for Savannah, this   day of August, 1737."

This the majority of the grand jury altered in some particulars, and on Thursday, September 1, delivered it again to the court, under the form of two presentments, containing ten bills, which were then read to the people.

Herein they asserted, upon oath, "That John Wesley, clerk, had broken the laws of the realm, contrary to the peace of our Sovereign Lord the King, his crown and dignity.

"1. By speaking and writing to Mrs. Williamson, against her husband's consent.

"2. By repelling her from the holy communion.

"3. By not declaring his adherence to the Church England.

"4. By dividing the morning service on Sundays.

"5. By refusing to baptize Mr. Parker's child, otherwise than by dipping, except the parents would certify it was weak, and not able to bear it.

"6. By repelling William Gough from the holy communion.

"7. By refusing to read the burial service over the body of Nathaniel Polhill.

"8. By calling himself Ordinary of Savannah.

"9. By refusing to receive William Aglionby as a godfather, only because he was not a communicant.

"10. By refusing Jacob Matthews for the same reason ; and baptizing an Indian trader's child with only two sponsors." (This, I own, was wrong ; for I ought, at all hazards, to have refused baptizing it till he had procured a third.)

Fri. Sep. 2.—Was the third court at which I appeared since my being carried before Mr. P. and the Recorder.

I now moved for an immediate hearing on the first bill, being the only one of a civil nature; but it was refused. I made the same motion in the afternoon, but was put off till the next court-day.

On the next court-day I appeared again, as also at the two courts following, but could not be heard, because (the Judge said) Mr. Williamson was gone out of town.

The sense of the minority of the grand jurors themselves (for they were by no means unanimous) concerning these presentments may appear from the following paper, which they transmitted to the trustees:

To the Honourable the Trustees for Georgia.

"Whereas two presentments have been made: the one of August 23, the other of August 31, by the grand jury for the town and county of Savannah, in Georgia, against John Wesley, Clerk.

"We, whose names are underwritten, being members of the said grand jury, do humbly beg leave to signify our dislike of the said presentments; being, by many and divers circumstances, thoroughly persuaded in ourselves that the whole charge against Mr. Wesley is an artifice of Mr. Causton's, designed rather to blacken the character of Mr. Wesley, than to free the colony from religious tyranny, as he was pleased, in his charge to us, to term it. But as these circumstances will be too tedious to trouble your Honours with, we shall only beg leave to give the reasons of our dissent from the particular bills. . . . .

Fri. Oct. 7.—I consulted my friends, whether God did not call me to return to England. The reason for which I left it had now no force; there being no possibility, as yet, of instructing the Indians; neither had I, as yet, found or heard of any Indians on the continent of America, who had the least desire of being instructed. And as to Savannah, having never engaged myself, either by word or letter, to stay there a day longer than I should judge convenient, nor ever taken charge of the people any otherwise than as in my passage to the heathens, I looked upon myself to be fully discharged therefrom, by the vacating of that design. Besides, there was a probability of doing more service to that unhappy people in England, than I could do in Georgia, by representing, without fear or favour, to the trustees the real state the colony was in. After deeply considering these things, they were unanimous, " that I ought to go; but not yet." So I laid the thoughts of it aside for the present; being persuaded, that when the time was come, God would "make the way plain before my face."

Why Wesley Left Georgia

Thur. Nov. 3.—I appeared again at the court, holden on that day; and again, at the court held Tuesday, November 22. On which day Mr. Causton desired to speak with me. He then read me some affidavits which had been made September 15, last past; in one of which it was affirmed, that I then abused Mr. Causton in his own house, calling him liar, villain, and so on. It was now likewise repeated before several persons, which indeed I had forgot, that I had been reprimanded at the last court, for an enemy to, and hinderer of, the public peace.

I again consulted my friends, who agreed with me, that the time we looked for was now come. And the next morning, calling on Mr. Causton, I told him, I designed to set out for England immediately. I set up an advertisement in the Great Square to the same effect and quietly prepared for my journey.

Fri. Dec. 2.—I proposed to set out for Carolina about noon, the tide then serving. But about ten, the magistrates sent for me, and told me, I must not go out of the province; for I had not answered the allegations laid against me. I replied, "I have appeared at six or seven courts successively, in order to answer them. But I was not suffered so to do, when I desired it time after time." Then they said, however, I must not go, unless I would give security to answer those allegations at their court. I asked, "What security?" After consulting together about two hours, the Recorder showed me a kind of bond, engaging me, under a penalty of fifty pounds, to appear at their court when I should be required. He added, "But Mr. Williamson too has desired of us, that you should give bail to answer his action." I then told him plainly, "Sir, you use me very ill, and so you do the trustees. I will give neither any bond, nor any bail at all. You know your business, and I know mine."

In the afternoon, the magistrates published an order, requiring all the officers and sentinels to prevent my going out of the province; and forbidding any person to assist me so to do. Being now only a prisoner at large, in a place where I know by experience, every day would give fresh opportunity to procure evidence of words I never said, and actions I never did; I saw clearly the hour was come for leaving this place : and as soon as evening prayers were over, about eight o'clock, the tide then serving, I shook off the dust of my feet, and left Georgia, after having preached the Gospel there (not as I ought, but as I was able) one year and nearly nine months.

Sat. 3.—We came to Purrysburg early in the morn
ing, and endeavoured to procure a guide to Port-
Royal.   But none being to be had, we set out without
one, an hour before sunrise.   After walking two or three
hours, we met with an old man, who led us into a small
path, near which was a line of blazed trees (that is,
marked by cutting off part of the bark), by following
which, he said, we might easily come to Port-Royal in
five or six hours.

Lost in the Woods

We were four in all; one of whom intended to go to
England with me; the other two to settle in Carolina.
About eleven we came into a large swamp, where we
wandered about till near two.   We then found another
blaze, and pursued it, till it divided into two: one of
these we followed through an almost impassable thicket,
a mile beyond which it ended.   We made through the
thicket again, and traced the other blaze till that ended
too.   It now grew toward sunset; so we sat down, faint
and weary, having had no food all day, except a ginger-
bread cake, which I had taken in my pocket.   A third
of this we had divided among us at noon; another third
we took now; the rest we reserved for the morning; but
we had met with no water all the day.   Thrusting a stick
into the ground, and finding the end of it moist, two of
our company fell a digging with their hands, and, at
about three feet depth, found water.   We thanked God,
drank, and were refreshed.   The night was sharp: however, there was no complaining among us; but after
having commended ourselves to God, we lay down
close together, and (I at least) slept till near six in the
morning.

Sun. 4.—God renewing our strength, we arose neither

faint nor weary, and resolved to make one trial more, to
find out a path to Port-Royal. We steered due east;
but finding neither path nor blaze, and the woods growing thicker and thicker, we judged it would be our best
course to return, if we could, by the way we came. The
day before, in the thickest part of the woods, I had broke
many young trees, I knew not why, as we walked along:
these we found a great help in several places, where no
path was to be seen; and between one and two God
brought us safe to Benjamin Arieu's house, the old man
we left the day before.

In the evening I read French prayers to a numerous
family, a mile from Arieu's; one of whom undertook to
guide us to Port-Royal. In the morning we set out.
About sunset, we asked our guide, if he knew where he
was; who frankly answered, "No." However, we pushed
on till, about seven, we came to a plantation; and the
next evening, after many difficulties and delays, we landed
on Port-Royal island.

Wed. 7.—We walked to Beaufort; where Mr. Jones,
the minister of Beaufort, with whom I lodged during my
short stay here, gave me a lively idea of the old English
hospitality. On Thursday Mr. Delamotte came; with
whom, on Friday, the 9th, I took boat for Charles-
Town. After a slow passage, by reason of contrary
winds, and some conflict (our provisions falling short)
with hunger as well as cold, we came thither early in the
morning, on Tuesday, the 13th.

Farewell to America

Thur. 22.—I took my leave of America (though,
if it please God, not for ever), going on board
the "Samuel," Captain Percy, with a young gentleman who had been a few months in Carolina, one of

my parishioners of Savannah, and a Frenchman, late
of Purrysburg, who was escaped thence with the skin
of his teeth.

Sat. 24.—We sailed over Charles-Town bar, and
about noon lost sight of land.

The next day the wind was fair, but high, as it was
on Sunday, 25, when the sea affected me more than
it had done in the sixteen weeks of our passage to
America. I was obliged to lie down the greatest part
of the day, being easy only in that posture.

Mon. 26.—I began instructing a Negro lad in the
principles of Christianity. The next day I resolved
to break off living delicately, and return to my old
simplicity of diet; and after I did so, neither my stomach
nor my head much complained of the motion of the
ship.

1738. Sun. Jan. 1.—All in the ship, except the captain
and steersman, were present both at the morning and
evening service, and appeared as deeply attentive as
even the poor people of Frederica did, while the word
of God was new to their ears. And it may be, one
or two among these likewise may " bring forth fruit with
patience."

Mon. 2.—Being sorrowful and very heavy (though I
could give no particular reason for it), and utterly
unwilling to speak close to any of my little flock (about
twenty persons), I was in doubt whether my neglect of
them was not one cause of my own heaviness. In the
evening, therefore, I began instructing the cabin-boy;
after which I was much easier.

I went several times the following days, with a design
to speak to the sailors, but could not. I mean, I was
quite averse from speaking; I could not see how to
make an occasion, and it seemed quite absurd to speak

without. Is not this what men commonly mean by, "I could not speak?" And is this a sufficient cause of silence, or no? Is it a prohibition from the good spirit? or a temptation from nature, or the evil one?

Sat. 7.—I began to read and explain some passages of the Bible to the young Negro. The next morning, another Negro who was on board desired to be a hearer too. From them I went to the poor Frenchman, who, understanding no English, had none else in the ship with whom he could converse. And from this time, I read and explained to him a chapter in the Testament every morning.

The Voyage to England

Fri. 13.—We had a thorough storm, which obliged us to shut all close; the sea breaking over the ship continually. I was at first afraid; but cried to God, and was strengthened. Before ten, I lay down: I bless God, without fear. About midnight we were awaked by a confused noise of seas and wind and men's voices, the like to which I had never heard before. The sound of the sea breaking over and against the sides of the ship, I could compare to nothing but large cannon, or American thunder. The rebounding, starting, quivering motion of the ship much resembled what is said of earthquakes.

The captain was upon deck in an instant. But his men could not hear what he said. It blew a proper hurricane; which beginning at south-west, then went west, north-west, north, and, in a quarter an hour, round by the east to the south-west point again. At the same time the sea running, as they term it, mountain-high, and that from many different points at once, the ship would not obey the helm; nor indeed could the steersman, through the violent rain, see the compass. So he was forced to let her run before the wind, and in half an hour the stress of the storm was over.

Tues. 24.—We spoke with two ships, outward-bound, from whom we had the welcome news of our wanting but one hundred and sixty leagues ot the Land's-end. My mind was now full of thought; part of which I writ down as follows:

"I went to America, to convert the Indians; but O! who shall convert me? who, what is he that will deliver me from this evil heart of mischief? I have a fair summer religion. I can talk well; nay, and believe myself, while no danger is near; but let death look me in the face, and my spirit is troubled. Nor can I say, 'To die is gain!'

'I have a sin of fear, that when I've spun
My last thread, I shall perish on the shore!'

"I think, verily, if the Gospel be true, I am safe: for I not only have given, and do give, all my goods to feed the poor; I not only give my body to be burned, drowned, or whatever God shall appoint for me; but I follow after charity (though not as I ought, yet as I can), if haply I may attain it. I now believe the Gospel is true. 'I show my faith by my works,' by staking my all upon it. I would do so again and again a thousand times, if the choice were still to make.

"Whoever sees me, sees I would be a Christian. Therefore 'are my ways not like other men's ways.' Therefore I have been, I am, I am content to be, 'a by-word, a proverb of reproach.' But in a storm I think, 'What, if the Gospel be not true? Then thou art of all men most foolish. For what hast thou given thy goods, thy ease, thy friends, thy reputation, thy country, thy life? For what art thou wandering over the face of the earth?—A dream! a cunningly-devised fable!'

"O! who will deliver me from this fear of death? What shall I do? Where shall I fly from it? Should I fight against it by thinking, or by not thinking of it? A wise man advised me some time since, 'Be still and go on.' Perhaps this is best, to look upon it as my cross; when it comes, to let it humble me, and quicken all my good resolutions, especially that of praying without ceasing; and at other times, to take no thought about it, but quietly to go on 'in the work of the Lord.'"

Lands at Deal

We went on with a small, fair wind, till Thursday in the afternoon; and then sounding, found a whitish sand at seventy-five fathom: but having had no observation for several days, the captain began to be uneasy, fearing we might either get unawares into the Bristol Channel, or strike in the night on the rocks of Scilly.

Sat. 28.—Was another cloudy day; but about ten in the morning, the wind continuing southerly, the clouds began to fly just contrary to the wind, and, to the surprise of us all, sunk down under the sun, so that at noon we had an exact observation; and by this we found we were as well as we could desire, about eleven leagues south of Scilly.

Sun. 29.—We saw English land once more; which, about noon, appeared to be the Lizard-Point. We ran by it with a fair wind; and at noon, the next day, made the west end of the Isle of Wight.

Here the wind turned against us, and in the evening blew fresh, so that we expected (the tide being likewise strong against us) to be driven some leagues backward

in the night: but in the morning, to our great surprise
we saw Beachy-Head just before us, and found we ha
gone forwards near forty miles.

Toward evening was a calm; but in the night a strong
north wind brought us safe into the Downs. The day
before, Mr. Whitefield had sailed out, neither of us then
knowing anything of the other. At four in the morning
we took boat, and in half an hour landed at Deal: it
being Wednesday, February 1, the anniversary festival
in Georgia for Mr. Oglethorpe's landing there.

It is now two years and almost four months since I
left my native country, and in order to teach the Georgian
Indians the nature of Christianity: but what have I
learned myself in the mean time? Why (what I the
least of all suspected), that I who went to America to
convert others, was never myself converted to God.*
"I am not mad," though I thus speak; but "I speak
the words of truth and soberness"; if haply some of
those who still dream may awake, and see, that as I am,
so are they.

In London Again

Wednesday, Feb. 1.—After reading prayers and explaining a portion of Scripture to a large company at the
inn, I left Deal, and came in the evening to Feversham.

I here read prayers, and explained the second lesson
to a few of those who were called Christians, but were
indeed more savage in their behaviour than the wildest
Indians I have yet met with.

Fri. 3.—I came to Mr. Delamotte's, at Blendon,
where I expected a cold reception. But God had prepared the way before me; and I no sooner mentioned

* I am not sure of this.

my name, than I was welcomed in such a manner as
constrained me to say : " Surely God is in this place, and
I knew it not ! Blessed be ye of the Lord ! Ye have
shown more kindness in the latter end than in the
beginning."

In the evening I came once more to London, whence
I had been absent two years and near four months.

Many reasons I have to bless God, though the design
I went upon did not take effect, for my having been
carried into that strange land, contrary to all my pre-
ceding resolutions. Hereby I trust He hath in some
measure " humbled me and proved me, and shown me
what was in my heart." Hereby I have been taught to
" beware of men." Hereby I am come to know assuredly
that if " in all our ways we acknowledge God, he will,"
where reason fails, " direct our path " by lot, or by the
other means which he knoweth. Hereby I am delivered
from the fear of the sea, which I had both dreaded and
abhorred from my youth.

Hereby God has given me to know many of his
servants ; particularly those of the Church of Hernhuth.
Hereby my passage is opened to the writings of holy
men in the German, Spanish, and Italian tongues. I
hope, too, some good may come to others hereby. All in
Georgia have heard the word of God. Some have
believed, and began to run well. A few steps have been
taken towards publishing the glad tidings both to the
African and American heathens. Many children have
learned "how they ought to serve God," and to be useful
to their neighbour. And those whom it most concerns
have an opportunity of knowing the true state of their
infant colony, and laying a firmer foundation of peace
and happiness to many generations.

Sat. 4.—I told my friends some of the reasons which

a little hastened my return to England. They all agreed
it would be proper to relate them to the trustees of
Georgia.

Accordingly, the next morning I waited on Mr. Oglethorpe, but had not time to speak on that head. In the
afternoon I was desired to preach at St. John the
Evangelist's. I did so on those strong words, " If any
man be in Christ, he is a new creature." I was afterwards informed many of the best in the parish were so
offended, that I was not to preach there any more.

Mon. 6.—I visited many of my old friends, as well as
most of my relations. I find the time is not yet come
when I am to be "hated of all men." O may I be
prepared for that day!

Wesley Meets Peter Böhler

Tues. 7.—(A day much to be remembered.) At the
house of Mr. Weinantz, a Dutch merchant, I met Peter
Böhler, Schulius Richter, and Wensel Neiser, just then
landed from Germany. Finding they had no acquaintance in England, I offered to procure them a lodging,
and did so near Mr. Hutton's, where I then was. And
from this time I did not willingly lose any opportunity
of conversing with them while I stayed in London.

Wed. 8.—I went to Mr. Oglethorpe again, but had no
opportunity of speaking as I designed. Afterwards I
waited on the Board of Trustees, and gave them a short
but plain account of the state of the colony : an account,
I fear, not a little differing from those which they had
frequently received before, and for which I have reason to
believe some of them have not forgiven me to this day.

Sun. 12.—I preached at St. Andrew's, Holborn, on :
" Though I give all my goods to feed the poor, and
though I give my body to be burned, and have not

C

charity, it profiteth me nothing." O hard sayings! Who can hear them? Here too, it seems, I am to preach no more.

Fri. 17.—I set out for Oxford with Peter Böhler, where we were kindly received by Mr. Sarney, the only one now remaining here of many who, at our embarking for America, were used to "take sweet counsel together," and rejoice in "bearing the reproach of Christ."

Sat. 18.—We went to Stanton-Harcourt. The next day I preached once more at the castle, in Oxford, to a numerous and serious congregation.

All this time I conversed much with Peter Böhler, but I understood him not; and least of all when he said, "My brother, my brother, that philosophy of yours must be purged away."

Mon. 20.—I returned to London. On Tuesday I preached at Great St. Helen's, on: "If any man will come after me, let him deny himself, and take up his cross daily, and follow me."

Sun. 26.—I preached at six, at St. Lawrence's; at ten, in St. Catherine Cree's church; and in the afternoon, at St. John's, Wapping. I believe it pleased God to bless the first sermon most, because it gave most offence; being, indeed, an open defiance of that mystery of iniquity which the world calls "prudence," grounded on those words of St. Paul to the Galatians, "As many as desire to make a fair show in the flesh, they constrain you to be circumcised; only lest they should suffer persecution for the cross of Christ."

Mon. 27.—I took coach for Salisbury, and had several opportunities of conversing seriously with my fellow travellers.

Tues. 28.—I saw my mother once more. The next day I prepared for my journey to my brother at Tiverton.

But on Thursday morning, March 2, a message that my brother Charles was dying at Oxford, obliged me to set out for that place immediately. Calling at an odd house in the afternoon, I found several persons there who seemed well-wishers to religion, to whom I spake plainly ; as I did in the evening both to the servants and strangers at my inn.

Wesley's Four Resolutions

With regard to my own behaviour, I now renewed and wrote down my former resolutions.

1. To use absolute openness and unreserve with all I should converse with.

2. To labour after continual seriousness, not willingly indulging myself in any the least levity of behaviour, or in laughter ; no, not for a moment.

3. To speak no word which does not tend to the glory of God ; in particular, not to talk of worldly things. Others may, nay, must. But what is that to thee ? And,

4. To take no pleasure which does not tend to th glory of God ; thanking God every moment for all I do take, and therefore rejecting every sort and degree of it, which I feel I cannot so thank him in and for.

Sat. March 4.—I found my brother at Oxford, recovering from his pleurisy ; and with him Peter Böhler ; by whom, in the hand of the great God, I was, on Sunday, the 5th, clearly convinced of unbelief, of the want of that faith whereby alone we are saved.

Immediately it struck into my mind, "Leave off preaching. How can you preach to others, who have not faith yourself?" I asked Böhler whether he thought I should leave it off or not. He answered, "By no means." I asked, "But what can I preach?" He said, "Preach faith till you have it; and then, because you have it, you will preach faith."

Accordingly, Monday, 6, I began preaching this new doctrine, though my soul started back from the work. The first person to whom I offered salvation by faith alone, was a prisoner under sentence of death. His name was Clifford. Peter Böhler had many times desired me to speak to him before. But I could not prevail on myself so to do; being still, as I had been many years, a zealous asserter of the impossibility of a death-bed repentance.

Incidents on the Manchester Road

Tues. 14.—I set out for Manchester with Mr. Kinchin, Fellow of Corpus Christi, and Mr. Fox, late a prisoner in the city prison.

About eight, it being rainy and very dark, we lost our way; but before nine, came to Shipston, having rode over, I know not how, a narrow foot-bridge, which lay across a deep ditch near the town. After supper I read prayers to the people of the inn, and explained the second lesson; I hope not in vain.

The next day we dined at Birmingham; and, soon after we left it, were reproved for our negligence there, in letting those who attended us go, without either exhortation or instruction, by a severe shower of hail.

In the evening we came to Stafford. The mistress of the house joined with us in family prayer. The next morning one of the servants appeared deeply affected, as did the ostler, before we went. Soon after breakfast, stepping into the stable, I spake a few words to those who were there. A stranger who heard me said, "Sir, I wish I was to travel with you"; and when I went into the house, followed me, and began abruptly, "Sir, I

believe you are a good man, and I come to tell you a
little of my life." The tears stood in his eyes all the
time he spoke; and we hoped not a word which was
said to him was lost.

At Newcastle, whither we came about ten, some to
whom we spoke at our inn were very attentive; but a
gay young woman waited on us, quite unconcerned :
however, we spoke on. When we went away, she fixed
her eyes and neither moved nor said one word, but
appeared as much astonished as if she had seen one
risen from the dead.

Coming to Holms-Chapel about three, we were surprised at being shown into a room where a cloth and
plates were laid. Soon after two men came in to dinner,
Mr. Kinchin told them, if they pleased, that gentleman
would ask a blessing for them. They stared and, as it
were, consented; but sat still while I did it, one of them
with his hat on. We began to speak on turning to God,
and went on, though they appeared utterly regardless.
After a while their countenances changed, and one of
them stole off his hat, and laying it down behind him,
said, all we said was true; but he had been a grievous
sinner, and not considered it as he ought; but he was
resolved, with God's help, now to turn to him in earnest.
We exhorted him and his companion, who now likewise
drank in every word, to cry mightily to God, that he
would " send them help from his holy place."

Late at night we reached Manchester.

Companions on Horseback

Fri. 17.—Early in the morning we left Manchester,
taking with us Mr. Kinchin's brother, for whom we came,
to be entered at Oxford. We were fully determined
to lose no opportunity of awakening, instructing, or

exhorting, any whom we might meet within our journey. At Knutsford, where we first stopped, all we spake to thankfully received the word of exhortation. But at Talk-on-the-hill, where we dined, she with whom we were was so much of a gentlewoman, that for near an hour our labour seemed to be in vain. However, we spoke on. Upon a sudden, she looked as one just awaked out of a sleep. Every word sunk into her heart. Nor have I seen so entire a change both in the eyes, face, and manner of speaking, of any one in so short a time.

About five, Mr. Kinchin riding by a man and woman double-horsed, the man said, " Sir, you ought to thank God it is a fair day; for if it rained, you would be sadly dirty with your little horse.' Mr. Kinchin answered, " True: and we ought to thank God for our life, and health, and food, and raiment, and all things." He then rode on, Mr. Fox following, the man said, " Sir, my mistress would be glad to have some more talk with that gentleman." We stayed, and when they came up, began to search one another's hearts. They came to us again in the evening, at our inn at Stone, where I explained both to them and many of their acquaintance who were come together, that great truth—godliness hath the promise both of this life and of that which is to come.

Tues. 21.—Between nine and ten we came to Hedgeford. In the afternoon one overtook us, whom we soon found more inclined to speak than to hear. However, we spoke, and spared not. In the evening we overtook a young man, a Quaker, who afterwards came to us, to our inn at Henley, whither he sent for the rest of his family, to join with us in prayer; to which I added, as usual, the exposition of the second lesson. Our other companion went with us a mile or two in the morning; and then not only spoke less than the day before, but took in good part a serious caution against talkativeness and vanity.

An hour after we were overtook by an elderly gentleman, who said he was going to enter his son at Oxford. We asked, "At what college?" He said he did not know; having no acquaintance there on whose recommendation he could depend. After some conversation, he expressed a deep sense of the good providence of God; and told us he knew God had cast us in his way, in answer to his prayer. In the evening we reached Oxford, rejoicing in our having received so many fresh instances of that great truth, "In all thy ways acknowledge Him, and He shall direct thy paths."

Preaches in Oxford Castle

Thur. 23.—I met Peter Böhler again, who now amazed me more and more, by the account he gave of the fruits of living faith—the holiness and happiness which he affirmed to attend it. The next morning I began the Greek Testament again, resolving to abide by "the law and the testimony"; and being confident that God would hereby show me whether this doctrine was of God.

Mon. 27.—Mr. Kinchin went with me to the castle, where, after reading prayers, and preaching on, "It is appointed unto men once to die," we prayed with the condemned man, first in several forms of prayer, and then in such words as were given us in that hour. He kneeled down in much heaviness and confusion, having "no rest in" his "bones, by reason of" his "sins." After a space he rose up, and eagerly said, "I am now ready to die. I know Christ has taken away my sins;

and there is no more condemnation for me." The same composed cheerfulness he showed when he was carried to execution; and in his last moments he was the same, enjoying a perfect peace, in confidence that he was "accepted in the Beloved."

Sun. April 2.—Being Easter-day, I preached in our college chapel, on, "The hour cometh, and now is, when the dead shall hear the voice of the Son of God, and they that hear shall live." I preached in the afternoon, first at the castle, and then at Carfax, on the same words. I see the promise; but it is afar off.

Believing it would be better for me to wait for the accomplishment of it in silence and retirement, on Monday 3, I complied with Mr. Kinchin's desire, and went to him at Dummer, in Hampshire. But I was not suffered to stay here long; being earnestly pressed to come up to London, if it were only for a few days. Thither, therefore, I returned, on Tuesday, 18th.

Talks with Böhler

I asked P. Böhler again, whether I ought not to refrain from teaching others. He said, "No; do not hide in the earth the talent God hath given you." Accordingly, on Tuesday 25, I spoke clearly and fully at Blendon to Mr. Delamotte's family, of the nature and fruits of faith. Mr. Broughton and my brother were there. Mr. Broughton's great objection was, he could never think that I had not faith, who had done and suffered such things. My brother was very angry, and told me, I did not know what mischief I had done by talking thus. And, indeed, it did please God then to kindle a fire, which I trust shall never be extinguished.

On Wednesday 26, the day fixed for my return to

Oxford, I once more waited on the trustees for Georgia; but, being straitened for time, was obliged to leave the papers for them, which I had designed to give into their own hands. One of these was the instrument whereby they had appointed me minister of Savannah; which, having no more place in those parts, I thought it not right to keep any longer.

P. Böhler walked with me a few miles, and exhorted me not to stop short of the grace of God. At Gerard's Cross I plainly declared to those whom God gave into my hands, the faith as it is in Jesus: as I did next day to a young man I overtook on the road, and in the evening to our friends at Oxford. A strange doctrine, which some, who did not care to contradict, yet knew not what to make of; but one or two, who were thoroughly bruised by sin, willingly heard, and received it gladly.

In the day or two following, I was much confirmed in the "truth that is after godliness," by hearing the experiences of Mr. Hutchins, of Pembroke College, and Mrs. Fox: two living witnesses that God can (at least, if he does not always) give that faith whereof cometh salvation in a moment, as lightning falling from heaven.

Mon. May 1.—The return of my brother's illness obliged me again to hasten to London. In the evening I found him at James Hutton's, better as to his health than I expected; but strongly averse from what he called "the new faith."

This evening our little society began, which afterwards met in Fetter-lane.

Wed. 3.—My brother had a long and particular conversation with Peter Böhler. And it now pleased God to open his eyes; so that he also saw clearly what was

the nature of that one true living faith, whereby alone,
" through grace, we are saved."

Thur. 4.—Peter Böhler left London, in order to
embark for Carolina. O what a work hath God begun,
since his coming into England! such an one as shall
never come to an end, till heaven and earth pass
away.

Sun. 7.—I preached at St. Lawrence's in the morning; and afterwards at St. Katherine Cree's church. I
was enabled to speak strong words at both ; and was
therefore the less surprised at being informed, I was not
to preach any more in either of those churches.

Sun. 14.—I preached in the morning at St. Ann's,
Aldersgate ; and in the afternoon at the Savoy Chapel,
free salvation by faith in the blood of Christ. I was
quickly apprised, that at St. Ann's, likewise, I am to
preach no more.

Fri. 19.—My brother had a second return of his
pleurisy. A few of us spent Saturday night in prayer.
The next day, being Whitsunday, after hearing Dr.
Heylyn preach a truly Christian sermon (on, " They
were all filled with the Holy Ghost ": " And so," said
he, " may all you be, if it is not your own fault "), and
assisting him at the holy communion (his curate being
taken ill in the church), I received the surprising news
that my brother had found rest to his soul. His bodily
strength returned also from that hour. " Who is so great
a God as our God ? "

I preached at St. John's, Wapping, at three, and at
St. Bennett's, Paul's-wharf, in the evening. At these
churches, likewise, I am to preach no more. At St.
Antholin's I preached on the Thursday following.

Monday, Tuesday, and Wednesday, I had continual sorrow and heaviness in my heart.

Wed. May 24.—I think it was about five this morning that I opened my Testament on those words, " There are given unto us exceeding great and precious promises, even that ye should be partakers of the divine nature " (2 Peter i. 4). Just as I went out, I opened it again on those words, " Thou art not far from the kingdom of God." In the afternoon I was asked to go to St. Paul's. The anthem was, " Out of the deep have I called unto thee, O Lord : Lord, hear my voice. O let thine ears consider well the voice of my complaint. If thou, Lord, wilt be extreme to mark what is done amiss, O Lord, who may abide it ? For there is mercy with thee ; therefore shalt thou be feared. O Israel, trust in the Lord : for with the Lord there is mercy, and with Him is plenteous redemption. And He shall redeem Israel from all his sins."

"I Felt my Heart Strangely Warmed"

In the evening I went very unwillingly to a society in Aldersgate-street, where one was reading Luther's preface to the Epistle to the Romans. About a quarter before nine, while he was describing the change which God works in the heart through faith in Christ, I felt my heart strangely warmed. I felt I did trust in Christ, Christ alone, for salvation ; and an assurance was given me that He had taken away my sins, even mine, and saved me from the law of sin and death.

I began to pray with all my might for those who had in a more especial manner despitefully used me and persecuted me. I then testified openly to all there what I now first felt in my heart. But it was not long before the enemy suggested, " This cannot be faith ; for where is thy joy?" Then was I taught that peace and victory over sin are essential to faith in the Captain of our salvation; but that, as to the transports of joy that usually attend the beginning of it, especially in those who have mourned deeply, God sometimes giveth, sometimes withholdeth them, according to the counsels of his own will.

After my return home, I was much buffeted with temptations; but cried out, and they fled away. They returned again and again. I as often lifted up my eyes, and He "sent me help from his holy place." And herein I found the difference between this and my former state chiefly consisted. I was striving, yea, fighting with all my might under the law, as well as under grace. But then I was sometimes, if not often, conquered; now, I was always conqueror.

Thur. 25.—The moment I awaked, "Jesus, Master," was in my heart and in my mouth; and I found all my strength lay in keeping my eye fixed upon him, and my soul waiting on him continually. Being again at St. Paul's in the afternoon, I could taste the good word of God in the anthem, which began, "My song shall be always of the loving-kindness of the Lord: with my mouth will I ever be showing forth thy truth from one generation to another." Yet the enemy injected a fear, "If thou dost believe, why is there not a more sensible change?" I answered (yet not I), "That I know not. But this I know, I have 'now peace with God.' And I sin not to-day, and Jesus my Master has forbid me to take thought for the morrow."

Wed. June 7.—I determined, if God should permit, to retire for a short time into Germany. I had fully proposed, before I left Georgia, so to do, if it should please God to bring me back to Europe. And I now clearly saw the time was come. My weak mind could not bear to be thus sawn asunder. And I hoped the conversing with those holy men who were themselves living witnesses of the full power of faith, and yet able to bear with those that are weak, would be a means, under God, of so establishing my soul, that I might go on from faith to faith, and from strength to strength."

[The next three months Wesley spent in Germany visiting the Moravians.]

Wesley Preaches in Newgate Gaol

Sun. September 17 (London).—I began again to declare in my own country the glad tidings of salvation, preaching three times, and afterwards expounding the holy Scripture, to a large company in the Minories. On Monday I rejoiced to meet with our little society, which now consisted of thirty-two persons.

The next day I went to the condemned felons, in Newgate, and offered them free salvation. In the evening I went to a society in Bear Yard, and preached repentance and remission of sins. The next evening I spoke the truth in love at a society in Aldersgate Street: some contradicted at first, but not long; so that nothing but love appeared at our parting.

Fri. Nov. 3.—I preached at St. Antholin's: Sunday, 5, in the morning, at St. Botolph's, Bishopsgate; in the afternoon, at Islington; and in the evening, to such a congregation as I never saw before, at St. Clement's, in the Strand. As this was the first time of my preaching here, I suppose it is to be the last.

Sun. Dec. 3 (Oxford).—I began reading prayers at Bocardo (the city prison), which had been long discontinued. In the afternoon I received a letter, earnestly desiring me to publish my account of Georgia; and

another, as earnestly dissuading me from it, "because it
would bring much trouble upon me." I consulted God in
His word, and received two answers: the first, Ezek. xxxiii.
2-6 : the other, "Thou therefore endure hardship, as a
good soldier of Jesus Christ."

Tues. 5.—I began reading prayers and preaching in
Gloucester Green workhouse; and on Thursday, in that
belonging to St. Thomas's parish. On both days I
preached at the castle. At St. Thomas's was a young
woman, raving mad, screaming and tormenting herself
continually. I had a strong desire to speak to her. The
moment I began she was still. The tears ran down her
cheeks all the time I was telling her, "Jesus of Nazareth
is able and willing to deliver you."

Mon. 11.—Hearing Mr. Whitefield was arrived from
Georgia, I hastened to London from Oxford; and on
Tuesday, 12, God gave us once more to take sweet
counsel together.

Wesley Begins Field-preaching

1739. March 15.—During my stay [in London] I was
fully employed; between our own society in Fetter Lane,
and many others, where I was continually desired to
expound ; so that I had no thought of leaving London,
when I received, after several others, a letter from Mr.
Whitefield, and another from Mr. Seward, entreating
me, in the most pressing manner, to come to Bristol
without delay. This I was not at all forward to do.

Wed. 28.—My journey was proposed to our society
in Fetter Lane. But my brother Charles would scarce
bear the mention of it; till appealing to the oracles of
God, he received those words as spoken to himself, and
answered not again: "Son of man, behold, I take from
thee the desire of thine eyes with a stroke: yet shalt

thou not mourn or weep, neither shall thy tears run down." Our other brethren, however, continuing the dispute, without any probability of their coming to one conclusion, we at length all agreed to decide it by lot. And by this it was determined I should go.

Thur. 29.—I left London, and in the evening expounded to a small company at Basingstoke. Saturday, 31. In the evening I reached Bristol, and met Mr. Whitefield there. I could scarce reconcile myself at first to this strange way of preaching in the fields, of which he set me an example on Sunday; having been all my life (till very lately) so tenacious of every point relating to decency and order, that I should have thought the saving of souls almost a sin, if it had not been done in a church.

April 1.—In the evening (Mr. Whitefield being gone) I begun expounding our Lord's sermon on the mount (one pretty remarkable precedent of field-preaching, though I suppose there were churches at that time also), to a little society which was accustomed to meet once or twice a week in Nicholas Street.

Mon. 2.—At four in the afternoon, I submitted to be more vile, and proclaimed in the highways the glad tidings of salvation, speaking from a little eminence in a ground adjoining to the city, to about three thousand people. The Scripture on which I spoke was this (is it possible any one should be ignorant, that it is fulfilled in every true minister of Christ?) "The Spirit of the Lord is upon me, because he hath anointed me to preach the Gospel to the poor ; he hath sent me to heal the broken-hearted; to preach deliverance to the captives, and recovery of sight to the blind; to set at liberty them that are bruised, to proclaim the accceptable year of the Lord."

Sun. 8.—At seven in the morning I preached to about a thousand persons at Bristol, and afterwards to about fifteen hundred on the top of Hannam-mount in Kingswood. I called to them, in the words of the evangelical Prophet, " Ho! every one that thirsteth, come ye to the waters; come, and buy wine and milk without money and without price." About five thousand were in the afternoon at Rose-green (on the other side of Kingswood); among whom I stood and cried, in the name of the Lord, " If any man thirst, let him come unto me and drink. He that believeth on me, as the Scripture hath said, out of his belly shall flow rivers of living water."

Tues. 17.—At five in the afternoon I was at a little society in the Back Lane. The room in which we were was propped beneath, but the weight of people made the floor give way; so that in the beginning of the expounding, the post which propped it fell down with a great noise. But the floor sunk no further; so that, after a little surprise at first, they quietly attended to the things that were spoken.

Mon. May 7.—I was preparing to set out for Pensford, having now had leave to preach in the church, when I received the following note:

" Sir,—Our minister, having been informed you are beside yourself, does not care you should preach in any of his churches."—I went, however; and on Priestdown, about half a mile from Pensford, preached Christ our " wisdom, righteousness, sanctification, and redemption."

Tues. 8.—I went to Bath, but was not suffered to be in the meadow where I was before, which occasioned the offer of a much more convenient place, where I preached Christ to about a thousand souls.

Wed. 9.—We took possession of a piece of ground near St. James's churchyard, in the Horse Fair, Bristol, where it was designed to build a room large enough to contain both the societies of Nicholas and Baldwin Street, and such of their acquaintance as might desire to be present with them, at such times as the Scripture was expounded. And on Saturday, 12, the first stone was laid with the voice of praise and thanksgiving.

The First Methodist Building

I had not at first the least apprehension or design of being personally engaged, either in the expense of this work, or in the direction of it, having appointed eleven feoffees, on whom I supposed these burdens would fall, of course ; but I quickly found my mistake. First, with regard to the expense : for the whole undertaking must have stood still, had not I immediately taken upon myself the payment of all the workmen ; so that before I knew where I was, I had contracted a debt of more than a hundred and fifty pounds. And this I was to discharge how I could; the subscriptions of both societies not amounting to one quarter of the sum.

And as to the direction of the work, I presently received letters from my friends in London, Mr. Whitefield in particular, backed with a message by one just come from thence, that neither he nor they would have anything to do with the building, neither contribute anything towards it, unless I would instantly discharge all feoffees, and do everything in my own name. Many reasons they gave for this ; but one was enough, viz., " that such feoffees always would have it in their power to control me; and, if I preached not as they liked, to turn me out of the room I had built." I accordingly yielded to their advice, and calling all the feoffees

D

together, cancelled (no man opposing) the instrument
made before, and took the whole management into my
own hands. Money, it is true, I had not, nor any human
prospect or probability of procuring it ; but I knew " the
earth is the Lord's, and the fulness thereof," and in his
name set out, nothing doubting.

Sun. 13.—My ordinary employment, in public, was
now as follows : Every morning I read prayers and
preached at Newgate. Every evening I expounded a
portion of Scripture at one or more of the societies.
On Monday, in the afternoon, I preached abroad, near
Bristol ; on Tuesday, at Bath and Two Mile Hill alter-
nately ; on Wednesday, at Baptist Mills ; every other
Thursday, near Pensford ; every other Friday, in another
part of Kingswood ; on Saturday in the afternoon, and
Sunday morning, in the Bowling-green (which lies
near the middle of the city) ; on Sunday, at eleven, near
Hannam-mount ; at two, at Clifton ; and at five on
Rose-green. And hitherto, as my days, so my strength
hath been.

Wesley's Living Arguments

Sun. 20.—Seeing many of the rich at Clifton church,
my heart was much pained for them, and I was earnestly
desirous that some even of them might " enter into the
kingdom of heaven." But full as I was, I knew not
where to begin in warning them to flee from the wrath
to come till my Testament opened on these words : " I
came not to call the righteous, but sinners to repentance " ; in applying which my soul was so enlarged that
methought I could have cried out (in another sense
than poor vain Archimedes), " Give me where to stand,
and I will shake the earth." God's sending forth
lightning with the rain did not hinder about fifteen

hundred from staying at Rose-green. Our Scripture was, "It is the glorious God that maketh the thunder. The voice of the Lord is mighty in operation; the voice of the Lord is a glorious voice." In the evening he spoke to three whose souls were all storm and tempest, and immediately there was a great calm.

During this whole time I was almost continually asked, either by those who purposely came to Bristol to inquire concerning this strange work, or by my old or new correspondents, "How can these things be?" And innumerable cautions were given me (generally grounded on gross misrepresentations of things), not to regard visions or dreams, or to fancy people had remission of sins because of their cries, or tears, or bare outward professions. To one who had many times wrote to me on this head, the sum of my answer was as follows:

"The question between us turns chiefly, if not wholly, on matter of fact. You deny that God does now work these effects; at least, that he works them in this manner. I affirm both, because I have heard these things with my own ears, and have seen with my eyes. I have seen (as far as a thing of this kind can be seen) very many persons changed in a moment from the spirit of fear, horror, despair, to the spirit of love, joy, and peace; and from sinful desire, till then reigning over them, to a pure desire of doing the will of God. These are matters of fact, whereof I have been, and almost daily am, an eye or ear witness.

What I have to say touching visions or dreams, is this: I know several persons in whom this great change was wrought in a dream, or during a strong representation to the eye of their mind, of Christ either on the cross or in the glory. This is the fact; let any judge of it as they please. And that such a change was then wrought appears (not from their shedding tears only, or falling into fit, or crying out; these are not the fruits, as you seem to suppose, whereby I judge, but) from the whole tenor of their life, till then many ways wicked; from that time holy, just, and good.

"I will show you him that was a lion till then, and is now a lamb; him that was a drunkard, and is now exemplarily sober; the whoremonger that was, who now abhors the very 'garment spotted by the flesh.' These are my living arguments for what I assert, viz., 'that God does now, as aforetime, give remission of sins and the gift of the Holy Ghost even to us and to our children; yea, and that always suddenly as far as I have known, and often in dreams or in the visions of God.' If it be not so, I am found a false witness before God. For these things I do, and by his grace, will testify."

Beau Nash Argues with Wesley

Tues. June 5.—There was great expectation at Bath of what a noted man was to do to me there; and I was much entreated not to preach, because no one knew what might happen. By this report I also gained a much larger audience, among whom were many of the rich and great. I told them plainly, the Scripture had concluded them all under sin—high and low, rich and poor, one with another. Many of them seemed to be a little surprised, and were sinking apace into seriousness, when their champion appeared, and coming close to me, asked by what authority I did these things.

I replied, "By the authority of Jesus Christ, conveyed to me by the (now) Archbishop of Canterbury, when he laid hands upon me, and said, 'Take thou authority to preach the Gospel.'" He said, "This is contrary to Act of Parliament: this is a conventicle." I answered,

" Sir, the conventicles mentioned in that Act (as the preamble shows) are seditious meetings; but this is not such; here is no shadow of sedition; therefore it is not contrary to that Act." He replied, " I say it is: and, beside, your preaching frightens people out of their wits."

" Sir, did you ever hear me preach ? " " No." " How, then, can you judge of what you never heard ? " " Sir, by common report." " Common report is not enough. Give me leave, Sir, to ask, Is not your name Nash ? " " My name is Nash." " Sir, I dare not judge of you by common report: I think it not enough to judge by." Here he paused awhile, and, having recovered himself, said, " I desire to know what this people comes here for ": on which one replied, " Sir, leave him to me: let an old woman answer him. You, Mr. Nash, take care of your body; we take care of our souls; and for the food of our souls we come here." He replied not a word, but walked away.

As I returned, the street was full of people, hurrying to and fro, and speaking great words. But when any of them asked, " Which is he ? " and I replied, " I am he," they were immediately silent. Several ladies following me into Mr. Merchant's house, the servant told me there were some wanted to speak to me. I went to them, and said, " I believe, ladies, the maid mistook: you only wanted to look at me." I added, " I do not expect that the rich and great should want either to speak with me, or to hear me; for I speak the plain truth—a thing you hear little of, and do not desire to hear." A few more words passed between us, and I retired.

Mon. 11.—I received a pressing letter from London (as I had several others before), to come thither as soon as possible; our brethren in Fetter Lane being in great confusion for want of my presence and advice. I therefore preached in the afternoon on these words: "I take you to record this day, that I am pure from the blood of all men; for I have not shunned to declare unto you all the counsel of God." After sermon I commended them to the grace of God, in whom they had believed. Surely God hath yet a work to do in this place. I have not found such love, no, not in England; nor so childlike, artless, teachable, a temper, as He hath given to this people.

Yet, during this whole time, I had many thoughts concerning the unusual manner of my ministering among them. But after frequently laying it before the Lord, and calmly weighing whatever objections I heard against it, I could not but adhere to what I had some time since wrote to a friend, who had freely spoken his sentiments concerning it. An extract of that letter I here subjoin that the matter may be placed in a clear light.

"All the World my Parish"

"You say, you cannot reconcile some parts of my behaviour with the character I have long supported. No, nor ever will. Therefore I have disclaimed that character on every possible occasion. I told all in our ship, all at Savannah, all at Frederica, and that over and over, in express terms, 'I am not a Christian; I only follow after, if haply I may attain it.'

.   .   .   .   .

'If you ask on what principle I acted, it was this: 'A desire to be a Christian; and a conviction that whatever I judge conducive thereto, that I am bound to do; wherever I judge I can best answer this end, thither it is my duty to go.' On this principle I set out for America; on this I visited the Moravian church; and on the same am I ready now (God being my helper) to go to Abyssinia or China, or whithersoever it shall please God, by this conviction, to call me.

"As to your advice that I should settle in college, I have no business there, having now no office, and no pupils. And whether the other branch of your proposal be expedient for me, viz., 'to accept of a cure of souls,' it will be time enough to consider when one is offered to me.

"But, in the meantime, you think I ought to sit still; because otherwise I should invade another's office, if I interfered with other people's business and intermeddled with souls that did not belong to me. You accordingly ask, 'How is it that I assemble Christians who are none of my charge, to sing psalms, and pray, and hear the Scriptures expounded?' and think it hard to justify doing this in other men's parishes, upon catholic principles?

"Permit me to speak plainly. If by catholic principles you mean any other than scriptural, they weigh nothing with me; I allow no other rule, whether of faith or practice, than the holy Scriptures. But on scriptural principles, I do not think it hard to justify whatever I do. God in Scripture commands me, according to my power, to instruct the ignorant, reform the wicked, confirm the virtuous. Man forbids me to do this in another's parish; that is, in effect, to do it at all; seeing I have now no parish of my own, nor probably ever shall. Whom then shall I hear, God or man?

. . . . . .

"I look upon all the world as my parish; thus far I mean, that, in whatever part of it I am, I judge it meet,

right, and my bounden duty, to declare unto all that are
willing to hear, the glad tidings of salvation. This is
the work which I know God has called me to; and sure
I am that his blessing attends it. Great encouragement
have I, therefore, to be faithful in fulfilling the work he
hath given me to do. His servant I am, and, as such,
am employed according to the plain direction of his
word, 'As I have opportunity, doing good unto all
men'; and his providence clearly concurs with his word;
which has disengaged me from all things else, that I
might singly attend on this very thing, 'and go about
doing good.'"

.   .   .   .   .

Susanna Wesley and her Son

Wed. 13.—After receiving the holy communion at
Islington, I had once more an opportunity of seeing my
mother, whom I had not seen since my return from
Germany.

I cannot but mention an odd circumstance here. I
had read her a paper in June last year, containing a
short account of what had passed in my own soul, till
within a few days of that time. She greatly approved
it, and said she heartily blessed God, who had brought
me to so just a way of thinking. While I was in
Germany a copy of that paper was sent (without my
knowledge) to one of my relations. He sent an account
of it to my mother, whom I now found under strange
fears concerning me, being convinced "by an account
taken from one of my own papers, that I had greatly
erred from the faith." I could not conceive what paper
that should be; but, on inquiry, found it was the same
I had read her myself. How hard is it to form a true
judgment of any person or thing from the account of a

prejudiced relater! yea, though he be ever so honest a
man: for he who gave this relation was one of unquestion-
able veracity. And yet by his sincere account of a
writing which lay before his eyes, was the truth so totally
disguised, that my mother knew not the paper she had
heard from end to end, nor I that I had myself wrote.

Thur. 14.—I went with Mr. Whitefield to Blackheath,
where were, I believe, twelve or fourteen thousand people.
He a little surprised me, by desiring me to preach in his
stead; which I did (though nature recoiled) on my
favourite subject, " Jesus Christ, who of God is made
unto us wisdom, righteousness, sanctification, and redemption."

I was greatly moved with compassion for the rich that
were there, to whom I made a particular application.
Some of them seemed to attend, while others drove
away their coaches from so uncouth a preacher.

Sun. 17.—I preached, at seven, in Upper-Moor-
fields, to (I believe) six or seven thousand people,
on, " Ho, every one that thirsteth, come ye to the
waters."

At five I preached on Kennington Common, to about
fifteen thousand people, on those words, " Look unto
me, and be ye saved, all ye ends of the earth."

Mon. 18.—I left London early in the morning, and
the next evening reached Bristol, and preached (as I
had appointed, if God should permit) to a numerous
congregation. My text now also was, " Look unto me
and be ye saved, all ye ends of the earth." Howell
Harris called upon me an hour or two after. He said,
he had been much dissuaded from either hearing or
seeing me, by many who said all manner of evil of me.
" But," said he, " as soon as I heard you preach, I
quickly found what spirit you was of. And before you

had done, I was so overpowered with joy and love, that I had much ado to walk home."

Sun. 24.—As I was riding to Rose-green, in a smooth, plain part of the road, my horse suddenly pitched upon his head, and rolled over and over. I received no other hurt than a little bruise on one side; which for the present I felt not, but preached without pain to six or seven thousand people on that important direction, "Whether ye eat or drink, or whatever you do, do all to the glory of God."

Talks with Whitefield

Fri. July 6.—In the afternoon I was with Mr. Whitefield, just come from London, with whom I went to Baptist Mills, where he preached concerning "the Holy Ghost, which all who believe are to receive"; not without a just, though severe, censure of those who preach as if there were no Holy Ghost.

Sat. 7.—I had an opportunity to talk with him of those outward signs which had so often accompanied the inward work of God. I found his objections were chiefly grounded on gross misrepresentations of matter of fact. But the next day he had an opportunity of informing himself better : for no sooner had he begun (in the application of his sermon) to invite all sinners to believe in Christ, than four persons sunk down close to him, almost in the same moment. One of them lay without either sense or motion. A second trembled exceedingly. The third had strong convulsions all over his body, but made no noise, unless by groans. The fourth, equally convulsed, called upon God, with strong cries and tears. From this time, I trust, we shall all suffer God to carry on his own work in the way that pleaseth him.

Fri. 13.—On Friday, in the afternoon, I left Bristol with Mr. Whitefield, in the midst of heavy rain. But the clouds soon dispersed, so that we had a fair, calm evening, and a serious congregation at Thornbury.

Tues. 17.—I rode to Bradford, five miles from Bath, whither I had been long invited to come. I waited on the minister, and desired leave to preach in his church. He said, it was not usual to preach on the week days; but if I could come thither on a Sunday, he should be glad of my assistance. Thence I went to a gentleman in the town, who had been present when I preached at Bath, and, with the strongest marks of sincerity and affection, wished me good luck in the name of the Lord. But it was past. I found him now quite cold. He began disputing on several heads; and at last told me plainly, one of our own college had informed him they always took me to be a little crack-brained at Oxford.

However, some persons who were not of his mind, having pitched on a convenient place (called Bear Field, or Bury Field), on the top of the hill under which the town lies; I there offered Christ to about a thousand people, for "wisdom, righteousness, sanctification, and redemption." Thence I returned to Bath, and preached on, "What must I do to be saved?" to a larger audience than ever before.

I was wondering the "god of this world" was so still; when, at my return from the place of preaching, poor R——d Merchant told me, he could not let me preach any more in his ground. I asked him why; he said, the people hurt his trees, and stole things out of his ground. "And besides," added he, "I have already, by letting thee be there, merited the displeasure of my neighbours." O fear of man! Who is above thee, but they who indeed "worship God in spirit and in truth?"

Not even those who have one foot in the grave! Not even those who dwell in rooms of cedar ; and who have heaped up gold as the dust, and silver as the sand of the sea.

Press-gang Disturbs the Sermon

Sat. 21.—I began expounding, a second time, our Lord's sermon on the mount. In the morning, Sunday, 22, as I was explaining, " Blessed are the poor in spirit," to about three thousand people, we had a fair opportunity of showing all men, what manner of spirit we were of : for in the middle of the sermon the press-gang came, and seized on one of the hearers (ye learned in the law, what becomes of Magna Charta, and of English liberty and property ? Are not these mere sounds, while, on any pretence, there is such a thing as a press-gang suffered in the land ?), all the rest standing still and none opening his mouth or lifting up his hand to resist them.

Mon. Sept. 3 (London).—I talked largely with my mother, who told me that, till a short time since, she had scarce heard such a thing mentioned, as the having forgiveness of sins now, or God's Spirit bearing witness with our spirit : much less did she imagine that this was the common privilege of all true believers. " Therefore," said she, " I never durst ask for it myself. But two or three weeks ago, while my son Hall was pronouncing those words, in delivering the cup to me, ' The blood of our Lord Jesus Christ, which was given for thee,' the words struck through my heart, and I knew God for Christ's sake had forgiven me all my sins."

I asked whether her father (Dr. Annesley) had not the same faith ; and, whether she had not heard him

preach it to others. She answered, he had it himself;
and declared, a little before his death, that for more than
forty years he had no darkness, no fear, no doubt at all
of his being "accepted in the Beloved." But that,
nevertheless, she did not remember to have heard him
preach, no, not once, explicitly upon it: whence she
supposed he also looked upon it as the peculiar blessing
of a few; not as promised to all the people of God.

The New Name of Methodism

Sun. 9.—I declared to about ten thousand, in Moorfields, what they must do to be saved. My mother went
with us, about five, to Kennington, where were supposed
to be twenty thousand people. I again insisted on that
foundation of all our hope, " Believe in the Lord Jesus,
and thou shalt be saved." From Kennington I went to
a society at Lambeth. The house being filled, the rest
stood in the garden. The deep attention they showed
gave me a good hope that they will not all be forgetful
hearers.

Sun. 16.—I preached at Moorfields to about ten
thousand, and at Kennington Common to, I believe,
near twenty thousand, on those words of the calmer Jews
to St. Paul, " We desire to hear of thee what thou
thinkest; for as concerning this sect, we know that
everywhere it is spoken against." At both places I
described the real difference between what is generally
called Christianity and the true old Christianity, which,
under the new name of Methodism, is now also everywhere spoken against.

Sun. 23.—I declared to about ten thousand, in Moorfields, with great enlargement of spirit, " The kingdom
of God is not meat and drink; but righteousness, and
peace, and joy in the Holy Ghost." At Kennington I

enforced to about twenty thousand that great truth, " One thing is needful." Thence I went to Lambeth, and showed (to the amazement, it seemed, of many who were present) how " he that is born of God doth not commit sin."

Mon. 24.—I preached once more at Plaistow, and took my leave of the people of that place. In my return, a person galloping swiftly rode full against me, and overthrew both man and horse ; but without any hurt to either. Glory be to Him who saves both man and beast !

An Accident and a Long Sermon

Thur. 27.—I went in the afternoon to a society at Deptford, and thence, at six, came to Turner's Hall: which holds (by computation) two thousand persons. The press both within and without was very great. In the beginning of the expounding, there being a large vault beneath, the main beam which supported the floor broke. The floor immediately sunk, which occasioned much noise and confusion among the people. But two or three days before, a man had filled the vault with hogsheads of tobacco. So that the floor, after sinking a foot or two, rested upon them, and I went on without interruption.

Sun. Oct. 7.—About eleven I preached at Runwick, seven miles from Gloucester. The church was much crowded, though a thousand or upwards stayed in the churchyard. In the afternoon I explained further the same words, " What must I do to be saved ? " I believe some thousands were then present, more than had been in the morning.

Between five and six I called on all who were present (about three thousand) at Stanley, on a little green, near the town, to accept of Christ, as their only " wisdom, righteousness, sanctification, and redemption." I was strengthened to speak as I never did before ; and continued speaking near two hours : the darkness of the night, and a little lightning, not lessening the number, but increasing the seriousness, of the hearers. I concluded the day by expounding part of our Lord's sermon on the mount, to a small, serious company at Ebly.

Wesley in Wales

Mon. 15.—Upon a pressing invitation, some time since received, I set out for Wales. About four in the afternoon I preached on a little green, at the foot of the Devauden (a high hill, two or three miles beyond Chepstow), to three or four hundred plain people, on " Christ our wisdom, righteousness, sanctification, and redemption." After sermon, one who I trust is an old disciple of Christ, willingly received us into his house : whither many following, I showed them their need of a Saviour, from these words, " Blessed are the poor in spirit." In the morning I described more fully the way to salvation —" Believe in the Lord Jesus, and thou shalt be saved " : and then, taking leave of my friendly host, before two came to Abergavenny.

I felt in myself a strong aversion to preaching here. However, I went to Mr. W—— (the person in whose ground Mr. Whitefield preached), to desire the use of it. He said, with all his heart—if the minister was not willing to let me have the use of the church : after whose refusal (for I wrote a line to him immediately), he invited me to his house. About a thousand people stood patiently (though the frost was sharp, it being after sunset), while, from Acts xxviii. 22, I simply described the plain, old religion of the Church of England, which is now almost everywhere spoken against, under the new name of Methodism.

Fri. 19.—I preached in the morning at Newport on "What must I do to be saved?" to the most insensible, ill-behaved people I have ever seen in Wales. One ancient man, during a great part of the sermon, cursed and swore almost incessantly; and, towards the conclusion, took up a great stone, which he many times attempted to throw. But that he could not do.—Such the champions, such the arms against field-preaching!

At four I preached at the Shire Hall of Cardiff again, where many gentry, I found, were present. Such freedom of speech I have seldom had, as was given me in explaining those words, "The kingdom of God is not meat and drink; but righteousness, and peace, and joy in the Holy Ghost." At six almost the whole town (I was informed) came together; to whom I explained the six last beatitudes: but my heart was so enlarged, I knew not how to give over, so that we continued three hours.

Sat. 20.—I returned to Bristol. I have seen no part of England so pleasant for sixty or seventy miles together as those parts of Wales I have been in. And most of the inhabitants are indeed ripe for the Gospel.

"A Terrible Sight"

Tues. 23.—In riding to Bradford I read over Mr. Law's book on the new birth. Philosophical, speculative, precarious: Behmenish, void, and vain!

"O what a fall is there!"

At eleven I preached at Bearfield to about three thousand, on the spirit of nature, of bondage, and of adoption.

Returning in the evening, I was exceedingly pressed

to go back to a young woman in Kingswood. (The fact I nakedly relate, and leave every man to his own judgment of it.)   I went.   She was nineteen or twenty years old ; but, it seems, could not write or read.   I found her on the bed, two or three persons holding her. It was a terrible sight.   Anguish, horror, and despair, above all description, appeared in her pale face.   The thousand distortions of her whole body showed how the dogs of hell were gnawing her heart.   The shrieks intermixed were scarce to be endured.   But her stony eyes could not weep.   She screamed out, as soon as words could find their way, " I am damned, damned ; lost for ever !   Six days ago you might have helped me. But it is past.   I am the devil's now.   I have given myself to him.   His I am.   Him I must serve.   With him I must go to hell.   I will be his.   I will serve him. I will go with him to hell.   I cannot be saved.   I will not be saved.   I must, I will, I will be damned ! "   She then began praying to the devil.   We began :

"Arm of the Lord, awake, awake ! "

She immediately sunk down as asleep; but, as soon as we left off, broke out again, with inexpressible vehemence : " Stony hearts, break !   I am a warning to you.   Break, break, poor stony hearts !   Will you not break?   What can be done more for stony hearts ?   I am damned that you may be saved.   Now break, now break, poor stony hearts !   You need not be damned, though I must."   She then fixed her eyes on the corner of the ceiling, and said : " There he is : ay, there he is ! Come, good devil, come !   Take me away.   You said you would dash my brains out : come, do it quickly.   I am yours.   I will be yours.   Come just now.   Take me away."

E

We interrupted her by calling again upon God : on which she sunk down as before : and another young woman began to roar out as loud as she had done. My brother now came in, it being about nine o'clock. We continued in prayer till past eleven ; when God in a moment spoke peace into the soul, first of the first tormented, and then of the other. And they both joined in singing praise to Him who had " stilled the enemy and the avenger."

"Yonder Comes Wesley, Galloping"

Sat. 27.—I was sent for to Kingswood again, to one of those who had been so ill before. A violent rain began just as I set out, so that I was thoroughly wet in a few minutes. Just at that time the woman (then three miles off) cried out, " Yonder comes Wesley, galloping as fast as he can." When I was come, I was quite cold and dead, and fitter for sleep than prayer. She burst out into a horrid laughter, and said, "No power, no power ; no faith, no faith. She is mine ; her soul is mine. I have her, and will not let her go."

We begged of God to increase our faith. Meanwhile her pangs increased more and more ; so that one would have imagined, by the violence of the throes, her body must have been shattered to pieces. One who was clearly convinced this was no natural disorder, said, " I think Satan is let loose. I fear he will not stop here." And added, " I command thee, in the name of the Lord Jesus, to tell if thou hast commission to torment any other soul." It was immediately answered, " I have. L——y C——r and S——h J——s." (Two who lived at some distance, and were then in perfect health.)

We betook ourselves to prayer again ; and ceased not

till she began, about six o'clock, with a clear voice and composed, cheerful look :

"Praise God, from whom all blessings flow."

Sun. 28.—I preached once more at Bradford, at one in the afternoon. The violent rains did not hinder more, I believe, than ten thousand from earnestly attending to what I spoke on those solemn words : "I take you to record this day that I am pure from the blood of all men. For I have not shunned to declare unto you all the counsel of God."

Returning in the evening, I called at Mrs. J——'s, in Kingswood. S——h J——s and L——y C——r were there. It was scarce a quarter of an hour before L——y C——r fell into a strange agony ; and presently after, S——h J——s. The violent convulsions all over their bodies were such as words cannot describe. Their cries and groans were too horrid to be borne, till one of them, in a tone not to be expressed, said : "Where is your faith now ? Come, go to prayers. I will pray with you. 'Our Father, which art in heaven.'" We took the advice, from whomsoever it came, and poured out our souls before God, till L——y C——r's agonies so increased, that it seemed she was in the pangs of death. But in a moment God spoke : she knew his voice ; and both her body and soul were healed.

We continued in prayer till near one, when S——h J——'s voice was also changed, and she began strongly to call upon God. This she did for the greatest part of the night. In the morning we renewed our prayers, while she was crying continually, "I burn ! I burn ! O what shall I do ? I have a fire within me. I cannot bear it. Lord Jesus ! Help !"—Amen, Lord Jesus ! when thy time is come.

Tues. Nov. 27.—I writ Mr. D. (according to his request) a short account of what had been done in Kingswood, and of our present undertaking there. The account was as follows:

"Few persons have lived long in the west of England who have not heard of the colliers of Kingswood; a people famous, from the beginning hitherto, for neither fearing God nor regarding man: so ignorant of the things of God, that they seemed but one remove from the beasts that perish; and therefore utterly without desire of instruction, as well as without the means of it.

The Colliers of Kingswood

"Many last winter used tauntingly to say of Mr. Whitefield, 'If he will convert heathens, why does not he go to the colliers of Kingswood?' In spring he did so. And as there were thousands who resorted to no place of public worship, he went after them into their own wilderness, 'to seek and save that which was lost.' When he was called away others went into 'the highways and hedges, to compel them to come in.' And, by the grace of God, their labour was not in vain. The scene is already changed. Kingswood does not now, as a year ago, resound with cursing and blasphemy. It is no more filled with drunkenness and uncleanness, and the idle diversions that naturally lead thereto. It is no longer full of wars and fightings, of clamour and bitterness, of wrath and envyings. Peace and love are there. Great numbers of the people are mild, gentle, and easy to be entreated. They 'do not cry, neither strive'; and hardly is their 'voice heard in the streets'; or, indeed, in their own wood; unless when they are at their usual evening diversion—singing praise unto God their Saviour.

"That their children too might know the things which make for their peace, it was some time since proposed to build a house in Kingswood; and after many foreseen and unforeseen difficulties, in June last the foundation was laid. The ground made choice of was in the middle of the wood, between the London and Bath roads, not far from that called Two Mile Hill, about three measured miles from Bristol.

"Here a large room was begun for the school, having four small rooms at either end for the schoolmasters (and, perhaps, if it should please God, some poor children) to lodge in. Two persons are ready to teach, so soon as the house is fit to receive them, the shell of which is nearly finished; so that it is hoped the whole will be completed in spring or early in the summer.

"It is true, although the masters require no pay, yet this undertaking is attended with great expense."

Wesley's Correspondents

1740. Thur. Jan. 3.—I left London, and the next evening came to Oxford, where I spent the two following days in looking over the letters which I had received for the sixteen or eighteen years last past. How few traces of inward religion are here! I found but one among all my correspondents who declared (what I well remember, at that time I knew not how to understand), that God had " shed abroad his love in his heart," and given him the " peace that passeth all understanding." But who believed his report? Should I conceal a sad truth, or declare it for the profit of others? He was expelled out of his society, as a madman; and, being disowned by his friends, and despised and forsaken of all men, lived obscure and unknown for a few months, and then went to Him whom his soul loved.

Mon. 21.—I preached at Hannam, four miles from Bristol. In the evening I made a collection in our congregation for the relief of the poor, without Lawford's gate; who, having no work (because of the severe frost), and no assistance from the parish wherein they lived, were reduced to the last extremity. I made another collection on Thursday; and a third on Sunday; by which we were enabled to feed a hundred, sometimes a hundred and fifty, a day, of those whom we found to need it most.

A Sermon and a Riot

Tues. April 1 (Bristol).—While I was expounding the former part of the twenty-third chapter of the Acts (how wonderfully suited to the occasion! though not by my choice), the floods began to lift up their voice. Some or other of the children of Belial had laboured to disturb us several nights before: but now it seemed as if all the host of the aliens were come together with one consent. Not only the court and the alleys, but all the street, upwards and downwards, was filled with people, shouting, cursing and swearing, and ready to swallow the ground with fierceness and rage. The mayor sent order that they should disperse. But they set him at nought. The chief constable came next in person, who was, till then, sufficiently prejudiced against us. But they insulted him also in so gross a manner, as I believe fully opened his eyes. At length the mayor sent several of his officers, who took the ringleaders into custody, and did not go till all the rest were dispersed. Surely he hath been to us " the minister of God for good."

Wed. 2.—The rioters were brought up to the court, the quarter sessions being held that day. They began to excuse themselves by saying many things of me. But the mayor cut them all short, saying, " What Mr. Wesley is, is nothing to you. I will keep the peace; I will have no rioting in this city."

Calling at Newgate in the afternoon, I was informed that the poor wretches under sentence of death were earnestly desirous to speak with me; but that it could not be; Alderman Beecher having just then sent an express order that they should not. I cite Alderman Beecher to answer for these souls at the judgment-seat of Christ.

Sun. Sep. 14 (London).—As I returned home in the evening, I had no sooner stepped out of the coach than the mob, who were gathered in great numbers about my door, quite closed me in. I rejoiced and blessed God, knowing this was the time I had long been looking for; and immediately spake to those that were next me of " righteousness, and judgment to come." At first not many heard, the noise round about us being exceeding great. But the silence spread farther and farther, till I had a quiet, attentive congregation; and when I left them, they all showed much love, and dismissed me with many blessings.

Preaching Incidents

Sun. 28.—I began expounding the sermon on the mount, at London. In the afternoon I described to a numerous congregation at Kennington, the life of God in the soul. One person who stood on the mount made a little noise at first; but a gentleman, whom I knew not, walked up to him, and, without saying one word, mildly took him by the hand and led him down. From that time he was quiet till he went away.

When I came home I found an innumerable mob round the door, who opened all their throats the

moment they saw me.   I desired my friends to go into
the house; and then walking into the midst of the
people, proclaimed, "the name of the Lord, gracious
and merciful, and repenting him of the evil."   They
stood staring one at another.   I told them they could
not flee from the face of this great God : and therefore
besought them, that we might all join together in crying
to Him for mercy.   To this they readily agreed : I then
commended them to his grace, and went undisturbed to
the little company within.

Tues. 30.—As I was expounding the twelfth of the
Acts, a young man, with some others, rushed in, cursing
and swearing vehemently; and so disturbed all near
him, that, after a time, they put him out.   I observed it,
and called to let him come in, that our Lord might bid
his chains fall off.   As soon as the sermon was over, he
came and declared before us all that he was a smuggler,
then going on that work; as his disguise, and the great
bag he had with him, showed.   But he said, he must
never do this more; for he was now resolved to have
the Lord for his God.

Wesley's Labour Colony

Tues. Nov. 25 (London).—After several methods proposed for employing those who were out of business, we
determined to make a trial of one which several of our
brethren recommended to us.   Our aim was, with as
little expense as possible, to keep them at once from
want and from idleness, in order to which, we took
twelve of the poorest, and a teacher, into the society-
room, where they were employed for four months, till
spring came on, in carding and spinning of cotton.   And
the design answered : they were employed and maintained
with very little more than the produce of their own labour.

Fri. 28.—A gentleman came to me full of good-will, to exhort me not to leave the Church; or (which was the same thing in his account) to use extemporary prayer; which, said he, " I will prove to a demonstration to be no prayer at all. For you cannot do two things at once. But thinking how to pray, and praying, are two things. *Ergo*, you cannot both think and pray at once." Now, may it not be proved by the self-same demonstration, that praying by a form is no prayer at all? *e.g.* " You cannot do two things at once. But reading and praying are two things. *Ergo*, you cannot both read and pray at once." Q.E.D.

Dispute with Whitefield

1741. Sun. Feb. 1.—A private letter, wrote to me by Mr. Whitefield, having been printed without either his leave or mine, great numbers of copies were given to our people, both at the door and in the Foundery itself. Having procured one of them, I related (after preaching) the naked fact to the congregation, and told them, " I will do just what I believe Mr. Whitefield would, were he here himself." Upon which I tore it in pieces before them all. Every one who had received it, did the same. So that in two minutes there was not a whole copy left.

Sat. March 28.—Having heard much of Mr. Whitefield's unkind behaviour, since his return from Georgia, I went to him to hear him speak for himself, that I might know how to judge. I much approved of his plainness of speech. He told me, he and I preached two different gospels; and therefore he not only would not join with, or give me the right hand of fellowship, but was resolved publicly to preach against me and my brother, wheresoever he preached at all. Mr. Hall (who went with me) put him in mind of the promise he had made but a few days before, that, whatever his private opinion was, he would never publicly preach against us. He said, that promise was only an effect of human weakness, and he was now of another mind.

Mon. April 6.—I had a long conversation with Peter Böhler. I marvel how I refrain from joining these men. I scarce ever see any of them but my heart burns within me. I long to be with them; and yet I am kept from them.

Thur. May 7.—I reminded the United Society that many of our brethren and sisters had not needful food; many were destitute of convenient clothing; many were out of business, and that without their own fault; and many sick and ready to perish: that I had done what in me lay to feed the hungry, to clothe the naked, to employ the poor, and to visit the sick; but was not, alone, sufficient for these things; and therefore desired all whose hearts were as my heart:

1. To bring what clothes each could spare to be distributed among those that wanted most.

2. To give weekly a penny, or what they could afford for the relief of the poor and sick.

My design, I told them, is to employ for the present all the women who are out of business, and desire it, in knitting.

To these we will first give the common price for what work they do; and then add, according as they need.

Twelve persons are appointed to inspect these, and to visit and provide things needful for the sick.

Each of these is to visit all the sick within their district every other day; and to meet on Tuesday evening, to give an account of what they have done, and consult what can be done farther.

Fri. 8.—I found myself much out of order. However, I made shift to preach in the evening : but on Saturday my bodily strength quite failed, so that for several hours I could scarce lift up my head. Sunday, 10. I was obliged to lie down most part of the day, being easy only in that posture. Yet in the evening my weakness was suspended, while I was calling sinners to repentance. But at our love-feast which followed, beside the pain in my back and head, and the fever which still continued upon me, just as I began to pray, I was seized with such a cough, that I could hardly speak. At the same time came strongly into my mind, "These signs shall follow them that believe." I called on Jesus aloud, to "increase my faith," and to "confirm the word of his grace." While I was speaking my pain vanished away; the fever left me; my bodily strength returned; and for many weeks I felt neither weakness nor pain. "Unto thee, O Lord, do I give thanks."

Wesl Northampton and Nottingham

Mon 8.—I set out from Enfield Chace for Leice In the evening we came to Northampton : and the next afternoon to Mr. Ellis's at Markfield, five or six miles beyond Leicester.

For these two days I had made an experiment which I had been so often and earnestly pressed to do—speaking to none concerning the things of God, unless my heart was free to it. And what was the event? Why, 1. That I spoke to none at all for fourscore miles together ; no, not even to him that travelled with me in the chaise, unless a few words at first setting out. 2. That I had no cross either to bear or to take up, and commonly, in an hour or two, fell fast asleep. 3. That I had much respect shown me wherever I came ; every one behaving to me, as to a civil, good-natured gentleman. O how pleasing is all this to flesh and blood! Need ye "compass sea and land" to make "proselytes" to this?

Sun. 14.—I rode to Nottingham, and at eight preached at the market-place, to an immense multitude of people, on, "The dead shall hear the voice of the Son of God; and they that hear shall live." I saw only one or two who behaved lightly, whom I immediately spoke to; and they stood reproved. Yet, soon after, a man behind me began aloud to contradict and blaspheme; but upon my turning to him, he stepped behind a pillar, and in a few minutes disappeared.

In the afternoon we returned to Markfield. The church was so excessive hot (being crowded in every corner), that I could not, without difficulty, read the evening service. Being afterwards informed that abundance of people were still without, who could not possibly get into the church, I went out to them, and explained that great promise of our Lord, "I will heal their backslidings: I will love them freely." In the evening I expounded in the church, on her who "loved much, because she had much forgiven."

Mon. 15.—I set out for London, and read over in the way that celebrated book, Martin Luther's "Comment on the Epistle to the Galatians." I was utterly ashamed. How have I esteemed this book, only because I heard it so commended by others; or, at best, because I had read some excellent sentences occasionally quoted from it! But what shall I say, now I judge for myself? now I see with my own eyes? Why, not only that the author makes nothing out, clears up not one considerable difficulty; that he is quite shallow in his remarks on many passages, and muddy and confused almost on all; but that he is deeply tinctured with mysticism throughout, and hence often dangerously wrong.

An Ox in the Congregation

Fri. July 10.—I rode to London, and preached at Short's Gardens, on, "the name of Jesus Christ of Nazareth." Sunday 12. While I was showing, at Charles' Square, what it is "to do justly, to love mercy, and to walk humbly with our God," a great shout began. Many of the rabble had brought an ox, which they were vehemently labouring to drive in among the people. But their labour was in vain; for in spite of them all, he ran round and round, one way and the other, and at length broke through the midst of them clear away, leaving us calmly rejoicing and praising God.

Sat. 25 (Oxford).—It being my turn (which comes about once in three years), I preached at St. Mary's, before the University. The harvest truly is plenteous. So numerous a congregation (from whatever motives they came) I have seldom seen at Oxford. My text was the confession of poor Agrippa, "Almost thou persuadest me to be a Christian." I have "cast my bread upon the waters." Let me "find it again after many days!"

Wed. Aug. 26 (London).—I was informed of a remarkable conversation, at which one of our sisters was present a day or two before; wherein a gentleman was assuring his friends, that he himself was in Charles Square, when a person told Mr. Wesley to his face, that he, Mr. Wesley, had paid twenty pounds already, on being convicted for selling Geneva; and that he now kept two Popish priests in his house. This gave occasion to another to mention what he had himself heard, at an eminent Dissenting teacher's, viz., that it was beyond dispute, Mr. Wesley had large remittances from Spain, in order to make a party among the poor; and that as soon as the Spaniards landed, he was to join them with twenty thousand men.

Wesley at Cardiff

Thur. Oct. 1.—We set out for Wales; but missing our passage over the Severn in the morning, it was sunset before we could get to Newport.   We inquired there if we could hire a guide to Cardiff; but there was none to be had.   A lad coming in quickly after, who was going (he said) to Lanissan, a little village two miles to the right of Cardiff, we resolved to go thither.   At seven we set out: it rained pretty fast, and there being neither moon nor stars, we could neither see any road, nor one another, nor our own horses' heads; but the promise of God did not fail; he gave his angels charge over us; and soon after ten we came safe to Mr. Williams's house at Lanissan.

Fri. 2.—We rode to Fonmon castle.   We found Mr. Jones's daughter ill of the small-pox; but he could cheerfully leave her and all the rest in the hands of Him in whom he now believed.   In the evening I preached at Cardiff, in the shire-hall, a large and convenient place, on, " God hath given unto us eternal life, and this life is in his Son."   There having been a feast in the town that day, I believed it needful to add a few words upon imtemperance: and while I was saying, " As for you, drunkards, you have no part in this life; you abide in death; you choose death and hell "; a man cried out vehemently, "I am one; and thither I am going."   But I trust God at that hour began to show him and others "a more excellent way."

Sun. Nov. 22 (Bristol).—Being not suffered to go to church as yet [after a serious fever], I communicated at home. I was advised to stay at home some time longer; but I could not apprehend it necessary : and therefore, on Monday, 23, went to the new room, where we praised God for all his mercies. And I expounded, for about an hour (without any faintness or weariness), on, "What reward shall I give upon the Lord for all the benefits that he hath done unto me? I will receive the cup of salvation, and call upon the name of the Lord."

I preached once every day this week, and found no inconvenience by it. Sunday, 29. I thought I might go a little farther. So I preached both at Kingswood and at Bristol; and afterwards spent near an hour with the society, and about two hours at the love-feast. But my body could not yet keep pace with my mind. I had another fit of my fever the next day; but it lasted not long, and I continued slowly to regain my strength.

A Curious Interruption

Mon. Dec. 7.—I preached on, "Trust ye in the Lord Jehovah; for in the Lord is everlasting strength." I was showing, what cause we had to trust in the Captain of our salvation, when one in the midst of the room cried out, "Who was your captain the other day, when you hanged yourself? I know the man who saw you when you was cut down." This wise story, it seems, had been diligently spread abroad, and cordially believed by many in Bristol. I desired they would make room for the man to come nearer. But the moment he saw the way open, he ran away with all possible speed, not so much as once looking behind him.

Sat. 12.—In the evening one desired to speak with me. I perceived him to be in the utmost confusion, so

that for awhile he could not speak. At length, he said,
" I am he that interrupted you at the new room, on
Monday. I have had no rest since, day or night, nor
could have till I had spoken to you. I hope you will
forgive me, and that it will be a warning to me all the
days of my life."

Wesley's Congregation Stoned

1742. Mon. Jan. 25 (London).—While I was explaining at Long Lane, " He that committeth sin is of
the devil "; his servants were above measure enraged:
they not only made all possible noise (although, as I had
desired before, no man stirred from his place, or answered them a word); but violently thrust many persons
to and fro, struck others, and break down part of the
house. At length they began throwing large stones
upon the house, which, forcing their way wherever they
came, fell down, together with the tiles, among the
people, so that they were in danger of their lives. I
then told them, "You must not go on thus; I am
ordered by the magistrate, who is, in this respect, to us
the minister of God, to inform him of those who break
the laws of God and the King: and I must do it if you
persist herein; otherwise I am a partaker of your sin."

When I ceased speaking they were more outrageous
than before. Upon this I said, " Let three or four
calm men take hold of the foremost, and charge a constable with him, that the law may take its course." They
did so, and brought him into the house, cursing and
blaspheming in a dreadful manner. I desired five or
six to go with him to Justice Copeland, to whom they
nakedly related the fact. The justice immediately
bound him over to the next sessions at Guildford.

I observed when the man was brought into the house,

that many of his companions were loudly crying out,
" Richard Smith, Richard Smith ! " who, as it afterwards appeared, was one of their stoutest champions.
But Richard Smith answered not; he was fallen into
the hands of One higher than they.   God had struck
him to the heart; as also a woman, who was speaking
words not fit to be repeated, and throwing whatever
came to hand, whom He overtook in the very act.   She
came into the house with Richard Smith, fell upon her
knees before us all, and strongly exhorted him, never to
turn back, never to forget the mercy which God had
shown to his soul.   From this time we had never any
considerable interruption or disturbance at Long Lane ;
although we withdrew our persecution, upon the offender's
submission and promise of better behaviour.

Tues. 26.—I explained at Chelsea the faith which
worketh by love.   I was very weak when I went into
the room ; but the more " the beasts of the people " increased in madness and rage, the more was I strengthened,
both in body and soul ; so that I believe few in the house,
which was exceeding full, lost one sentence of what I
spoke.   Indeed they could not see me, nor one another
at a few yards distance, by reason of the exceeding thick
smoke, which was occasioned by the wild-fire, and things
of that kind, continually thrown into the room.   But
they who could praise God in the midst of the fires were
not to be affrighted by a little smoke.

Mon. Feb. 15.—Many met together to consult on a
proper method for discharging the public debt ; and it
was at length agreed, 1. That every member of the
society, who was able, should contribute a penny a week.
2. That the whole society should be divided into little
companies or classes—about twelve in each class.   And
3. That one person in each class should receive the

contribution of the rest, and bring it in to the Stewards,
weekly.

Fri. March 10.—I rode once more to Pensford at
the earnest request of several serious people.   The place
where they desired me to preach was a little green spot,
near the town.   But I had no sooner begun than a great
company of rabble, hired (as we afterwards found) for
that purpose, came furiously upon us, bringing a bull,
which they had been baiting, and now strove to drive in
among the people.   But the beast was wiser than his
drivers; and continually ran either on one side of us or
the other, while we quietly sang praise to God, and
prayed for about an hour.   The poor wretches, finding
themselves disappointed, at length seized upon the bull,
now weak and tired, after having been so long torn and
beaten both by dogs and men; and, by main strength,
partly dragged, and partly thrust, him in among the
people.

A Bull in the Congregation

When they had forced their way to the little table on
which I stood, they strove several times to throw it down,
by thrusting the helpless beast against it, who, of himself, stirred no more than a log of wood.   I once or
twice put aside his head with my hand, that the blood
might not drop upon my clothes; intending to go on as
soon as the hurry should be a little over.   But the table
falling down, some of our friends caught me in their
arms, and carried me right away on their shoulders; while
the rabble wreaked their vengeance on the table, which
they tore bit from bit.   We went a little way off, where I
finished my discourse, without any noise or interruption.

Sun. 21.—In the evening I rode to Marshfield, and
on Tuesday, in the afternoon, came to London.   Wed-

nesday, 24. I preached for the last time in the French chapel at Wapping, on "If ye continue in my word, then are ye my disciples indeed."

Thur. 25.—I appointed several earnest and sensible men to meet me, to whom I showed the great difficulty I had long found of knowing the people who desired to be under my care. After much discourse, they all agreed, there could be no better way to come to a sure, thorough knowledge of each person, than to divide them into classes, like those at Bristol, under the inspection of those in whom I could most confide. This was the origin of our classes at London, for which I can never sufficiently praise God; the unspeakable usefulness of the institution having ever since been more and more manifest.

Fri. April 9.—We had the first watch-night in London. We commonly choose for this solemn service the Friday night nearest the full moon, either before or after, that those of the congregation who live at a distance, may have light to their several homes. The service begins at half an hour past eight, and continues till a little after midnight. We have often found a peculiar blessing at these seasons. There is generally a deep awe upon the congregation, perhaps in some measure owing to the silence of the night, particularly in singing the hymn with which we commonly conclude :

> " Hearken to the solemn voice,
>   The awful midnight cry !
> Waiting souls, rejoice, rejoice,
>   And feel the Bridegroom nigh."

Sun. May 9.—I preached in Charles Square to the largest congregation I have ever seen there. Many of the baser people would fain have interrupted, but they found, after a time, it was lost labour. One, who was more serious, was (as she afterwards confessed) exceedingly angry at them. But she was quickly rebuked, by a stone which light upon her forehead, and struck her down to the ground. In that moment her anger was at an end, and love only filled her heart.

Wed. 12.—I waited on the Archbishop of Canterbury with Mr. Whitefield, and again on Friday; as also on the Bishop of London. I trust if we should be called to appear before princes, we should not be ashamed.

Wesley Was "the Better Mounted"

Mon. 17.—I had designed this morning to set out for Bristol; but was unexpectedly prevented. In the afternoon I received a letter from Leicestershire, pressing me to come without delay, and pay the last office of friendship to one whose soul was on the wing for eternity. On Thursday, 20, I set out. The next afternoon I stopped a little at Newport-Pagnell, and then rode on till I overtook a serious man, with whom I immediately fell into conversation.

He presently gave me to know what his opinions were : therefore I said nothing to contradict them. But that did not content him : he was quite uneasy to know whether I held the doctrine of the decrees as he did; but I told him over and over, " We had better keep to practical things, lest we should be angry at one another." And so we did for two miles, till he caught me unawares, and dragged me into the dispute before I knew where I was. He then grew warmer and warmer; told me I was rotten at heart, and supposed I was one of John Wesley's followers. I told him, " No, I am John Wesley himself." Upon which he would gladly have run away outright. But being the better mounted of the two, I kept close to his side, and endeavoured to show him his heart, till we came into the street of Northampton.

Thur. 27.—We came to Newcastle about six; and, after a short refreshment, walked into the town. I was surprised : so much drunkenness, cursing, and swearing (even from the mouths of little children), do I never remember to have seen and heard before, in so small a compass of time. Surely this place is ripe for Him who " came not to call the righteous, but sinners to repentance."

Sun. 30.—At seven I walked down to Sandgate, the poorest and most contemptible part of the town ; and, standing at the end of the street with John Taylor, began to sing the hundredth Psalm. Three or four people came out to see what was the matter ; who soon increased to four or five hundred. I suppose there might be twelve or fifteen hundred, before I had done preaching ; to whom I applied those solemn words, " He was wounded for our transgressions, He was bruised for our iniquities ; the chastisement of our peace was upon Him ; and by His stripes we are healed."

A Big Crowd at Newcastle

Observing the people, when I had done, to stand gaping and staring upon me, with the most profound astonishment, I told them, " If you desire to know who I am, my name is John Wesley. At five in the evening, with God's help, I design to preach here again."

At five, the hill on which I designed to preach was covered, from the top to the bottom. I never saw so large a number of people together, either at Moorfields, or at Kennington Common. I knew it was not possible for the one half to hear, although my voice was then strong and clear ; and I stood so as to have them all in view, as they were ranged on the side of the hill. The word of God which I set before them was, " I will heal their backsliding, I will love them freely." After preaching, the poor people were ready to tread me under foot, out of pure love and kindness. It was some time before I could possibly get out of the press. I then went back another way than I come; but several were got to our inn before me; by whom I was vehemently importuned to stay with them, at least, a few days; or, however, one day more. But I could not consent; having given my word to be at Birstal, with God's leave, on Tuesday night.

Wesley on his Father's Tombstone

Sat. June 5.—It being many years since I had been in Epworth before, I went to an inn, in the middle of the town, not knowing whether there were any left in it now who would not be ashamed of my acquaintance. But an old servant of my father's, with two or three poor women, presently found me out. I asked her, " Do you know any in Epworth who are in earnest to be saved?" She answered, "I am, by the grace of God; and I know I am saved through faith." I asked, " Have you then the peace of God? Do you know that He has forgiven your sins?" She replied, "I thank God, I know it well. And many here can say the same thing."

Sun. 6.—A little before the service began, I went to Mr. Romley, the curate, and offered to assist him either by preaching or reading prayers. But he did not care to accept of my assistance. The church was exceeding full in the afternoon, a rumour being spread that I was to preach. But the sermon on, "Quench not the Spirit," was not suitable to the expectation of many of the hearers. Mr. Romley told them, one of the most dangerous ways of quenching the Spirit was by enthusiasm; and enlarged on the character of an enthusiast, in a very florid and oratorical manner. After sermon John Taylor stood in the churchyard, and gave notice, as the people were coming out, " Mr. Wesley, not being permitted to preach in the church, designs to preach here at six o'clock."

Accordingly at six I came, and found such a congregation as I believe Epworth never saw before. I stood near the east end of the church, upon my father's tombstone, and cried, " The kingdom of heaven is not meat and drink ; but righteousness, and peace, and joy in the Holy Ghost."

"Let them Convert the Scolds"

Wed. 9.—I rode over to a neighbouring town, to wait upon a justice of peace, a man of candour and understanding ; before whom (I was informed) their angry neighbours had carried a whole waggon-load of these new heretics. But when he asked what they had done, there was a deep silence ; for that was a point their conductors had forgot. At length one said, " Why, they pretended to be better than other people ; and besides, they prayed from morning to night." Mr. S. asked, " But have they done nothing besides ? " " Yes, sir," said an old man : " an't please your worship. they have *convarted* my wife. Till she went among them, she had such a tongue ! And now she is as quiet as a lamb." " Carry them back, carry them back," replied the justice, "and let them convert all the scolds in the town."

Sat. 12.—I preached on the righteousness of the law and the righteousness of faith. While I was speaking, several dropped down as dead ; and among the rest, such a cry was heard, of sinners groaning for the

righteousness of faith, as almost drowned my voice.
But many of these soon lifted up their heads with joy,
and broke out into thanksgiving; being assured they
now had the desire of their soul—the forgiveness of
their sins.

I observed a gentleman there, who was remarkable
for not pretending to be of any religion at all. I was
informed he had not been at public worship of any kind
for upwards of thirty years. Seeing him stand as
motionless as a statue, I asked him abruptly, " Sir, are
you a sinner ? " He replied, with a deep and broken
voice, " Sinner enough "; and continued staring upwards
till his wife and a servant or two, who were all in tears,
put him into his chaise and carried him home.

Sun. 13.—At seven I preached at Haxey, on, " What
must I do to be saved ? " Thence I went to Wroote, of
which (as well as Epworth) my father was rector for
several years. Mr. Whitelamb offering me the church, I
preached in the morning on, " Ask, and it shall be given
you " : in the afternoon, on the difference between the
righteousness of the law and the righteousness of faith.
But the church could not contain the people, many of
whom came from far, and, I trust, not in vain.

At six I preached for the last time in Epworth churchyard (being to leave the town the next morning), to a
vast multitude gathered together from all parts, on the
beginning of our Lord's Sermon on the Mount. I continued among them for near three hours, and yet we
scarce knew how to part. O let none think his labour
of love is lost because the fruit does not immediately
appear ! Near forty years did my father labour here ;
but he saw little fruit of all his labour. I took some
pains among this people too ; and my strength also
seemed spent in vain ; but now the fruit appeared.

There were scarce any in the town on whom either my
father or I had taken any pains formerly but the seed,
sown so long since, now sprung up, bringing forth repentance and remission of sins.

Death of Wesley's Mother

I left Bristol in the evening of Sunday, July 18, and
on Tuesday came to London. I found my mother on
the borders of eternity. But she had no doubt or fear;
nor any desire but (as soon as God should call) "to
depart and be with Christ."

Fri. 23.—About three in the afternoon I went to my
mother, and found her change was near. I sat down on
the bed-side. She was in her last conflict; unable to
speak, but I believe quite sensible. Her look was calm
and serene, and her eyes fixed upward, while we commended her soul to God. From three to four the silver
cord was loosing, and the wheel breaking at the cistern;
and then without any struggle, or sigh, or groan, the
soul was set at liberty. We stood round the bed, and
fulfilled her last request, uttered a little before she lost
her speech: "Children, as soon as I am released, sing a
psalm of praise to God."

Sun. August 1.—Almost an innumerable company of
people being gathered together, about five in the afternoon, I committed to the earth the body of my mother,
to sleep with her fathers. The portion of Scripture
from which I afterwards spoke was, "I saw a great
white throne, and Him that sat on it, from whose face
the earth and the heaven fled away; and there was
found no place for them. And I saw the dead, small
and great, stand before God; and the books were
opened : and the dead were judged out of those things
which were written in the books, according to their

works." It was one of the most solemn assemblies I ever saw, or expect to see on this side eternity.

We set up a plain stone at the head of her grave, inscribed with the following words :

Here lies the Body

OF

MRS. SUSANNAH WESLEY,

THE YOUNGEST AND LAST SURVIVING DAUGHTER OF
DR. SAMUEL ANNESLEY.

In sure and steadfast hope to rise,
And claim her mansion in the skies,
A Christian here her flesh laid down,
The cross exchanging for a crown.

True daughter of affliction, she,
Inured to pain and misery,
Mourn'd a long night of griefs and fears,
A legal night of seventy years.

The Father then reveal'd his Son,
Him in the broken bread made known,
She knew and felt her sins forgiven,
And found the earnest of her heaven.

Meet for the fellowship above,
She heard the call, "Arise, my love!"
"I come," her dying looks replied,
And lamb-like, as her Lord, she died.

Mrs. Wesley as Preacher

I cannot but further observe, that even she (as well as her father, and grandfather, her husband, and her three sons) had been, in her measure and degree, a preacher of righteousness. This I learned from a letter, wrote long since to my father ; part of which I have here subjoined :

February 6, 1711–12.

" —— As I am a woman, so I am also mistress of a large family. And though the superior charge of the souls contained in it lies upon you; yet, in your absence, I cannot but look upon every soul you leave under my care, as a talent committed to me under a trust, by the great Lord of all the families both of heaven and earth. And if I am unfaithful to him or you in neglecting to improve these talents, how shall I answer unto him, when he shall command me to render an account of my stewardship?

" As these, and other such like thoughts, made me at first take a more than ordinary care of the souls of my children and servants, so—knowing our religion requires a strict observation of the Lord's day, and not thinking that we fully answered the end of the institution by going to church, unless we filled up the intermediate spaces of time by other acts of piety and devotion—I thought it my duty to spend some part of the day, in reading to and instructing my family: and such time I esteemed spent in a way more acceptable to God, than if I had retired to my own private devotions.

" This was the beginning of my present practice. Other people's coming and joining with us was merely accidental. Our lad told his parents: they first desired to be admitted; then others that heard of it begged leave also: so our company increased to about thirty; and it seldom exceeded forty last winter.

" But soon after you went to London last, I light on the account of the Danish Missionaries. I was, I think, never more affected with anything; I could not forbear spending good part of that evening in praising and adoring the divine goodness for inspiring them with such ardent zeal for His glory. For several days I could think or speak of little else. At last it came into my mind, Though I am not a man nor a minister, yet if my heart were sincerely devoted to God, and I was

inspired with a true zeal for his glory, I might do
somewhat more than I do. I thought I might pray
more for them, and might speak to those with whom I
converse with more warmth of affection. I resolved to
begin with my own children; in which I observe the
following method: I take such a proportion of time as I
can spare every night to discourse with each child apart.
On Monday, I talk with Molly; on Tuesday, with Hetty;
Wednesday, with Nancy; Thursday, with Jacky; Friday,
with Patty; Saturday, with Charles; and with Emily and
Suky together on Sunday.

She Speaks to Two Hundred

"With those few neighbours that then came to me, I
discoursed more freely and affectionately. I chose the
best and most awakening sermons we have. And I
spent somewhat more time with them in such exercises,
without being careful about the success of my undertaking. Since this, our company increased every night;
for I dare deny none that ask admittance."

"Last Sunday I believe we had above two hundred.
And yet many went away, for want of room to stand.

"We banish all temporal concerns from our society.
None is suffered to mingle any discourse about them
with our reading or singing. We keep close to the
business of the day; and when it is over, all go home.

"I cannot conceive, why any should reflect upon you,
because your wife endeavours to draw people to church,
and to restrain them from profaning the Lord's day, by
reading to them, and other persuasions. For my part,
I value no censure upon this account. I have long
since shook hands with the world. And I heartily
wish, I had never given them more reason to speak
against me.

"As to its looking particular, I grant it does. And so does almost anything that is serious, or that may any way advance the glory of God, or the salvation of souls.

"As for your proposal, of letting some other person read : alas ! you do not consider what a people these are. I do not think one man among them could read a sermon, without spelling a good part of it. Nor has any of our family a voice strong enough to be heard by such a number of people.

"But there is one thing about which I am much dissatisfied ; that is, their being present at family prayers. I do not speak of any concern I am under, barely because so many are present ; for those who have the honour of speaking to the Great and Holy God, need not be ashamed to speak before the whole world ; but because of my sex. I doubt if it is proper for me to present the prayers of the people to God. Last Sunday I would fain have dismissed them before prayers ; but they begged so earnestly to stay, I durst not deny them.

"To the Rev. Mr. Wesley,
   "In St. Margaret's Churchyard, Westminster."

How the Wesleys were Brought up

For the benefit of those who are entrusted, as she was, with the care of a numerous family, I cannot but add one letter more, which I received many years ago :

July 24, 1732.

"Dear Son,—According to your desire, I have collected the principal rules I observed in educating my family ; which I now send you as they occurred to my mind, and you may (if you think they can be of use to any) dispose of them in what order you please.

" The children were always put into a regular method of living, in such things as they were capable of, from their birth; as in dressing, undressing, changing their linen, &c. The first quarter commonly passes in sleep. After that, they were, if possible, laid into their cradles awake, and rocked to sleep; and so they were kept rocking, till it was time for them to awake. This was done to bring them to a regular course of sleeping; which at first was three hours in the morning, and three in the afternoon: afterward two hours, till they needed none at all.

" When turned a year old (and some before), they were taught to fear the rod, and to cry softly; by which means they escaped abundance of correction they might otherwise have had; and that most odious noise of the crying of children was rarely heard in the house; but the family usually lived in as much quietness as if there had not been a child among them.

" As soon as they were grown pretty strong, they were confined to three meals a day. At dinner their little table and chairs were set by ours, where they could be overlooked; and they were suffered to eat and drink (small beer) as much as they would; but not to call for anything. If they wanted aught, they used to whisper to the maid which attended them, who came and spake to me; and as soon as they could handle a knife and fork, they were set to our table. They were never suffered to choose their meat, but always made to eat such things as were provided for the family.

" Mornings they had always spoon-meat; sometimes at nights. But whatever they had, they were never permitted to eat, at those meals, of more than one thing; and of that sparingly enough. Drinking or eating between meals was never allowed, unless in case of sickness; which seldom happened. Nor were they suffered to go into the kitchen to ask anything of the servants, when they were at meat: if it was known they did, they were certainly beat, and the servants severely reprimanded.

" At six, as soon as family prayers were over, they had their supper; at seven, the maid washed them; and, beginning at the youngest, she undressed and got them all to bed by eight; at which time she left them in their several rooms awake; for there was no such thing allowed of in our house, as sitting by a child till it fell asleep.

" They were so constantly used to eat and drink what was given them, that when any of them was ill, there was no difficulty in making them take the most unpleasant medicine: for they durst not refuse it, though some of them would presently throw it up. This I mention to show that a person may be taught to take anything, though it be never so much against his stomach.

"Conquer the Child's Will"

" In order to form the minds of children, the first thing to be done is to conquer their will, and bring them to an obedient temper. To inform the understanding is a work of time, and must with children proceed by slow degrees as they are able to bear it : but the subjecting the will is a thing which must be done at once; and the sooner the better. For by neglecting timely correction, they will contract a stubbornness and obstinacy which is hardly ever after conquered; and never, without using such severity as would be as painful to me as to the child. In the esteem of the world they pass for kind and indulgent, whom I call cruel, parents, who

permit their children to get habits which they know
must be afterwards broken. Nay, some are so stupidly
fond, as in sport to teach their children to do things
which, in a while after, they have severely beaten them
for doing.

"Whenever a child is corrected, it must be conquered;
and this will be no hard matter to do, if it be not grown
headstrong by too much indulgence. And when the
will of a child is totally subdued, and it is brought to
revere and stand in awe of the parents, then a great
many childish follies and inadvertences may be passed
by. Some should be overlooked and taken no notice
of, and others mildly reproved; but no wilful trans-
gression ought ever to be forgiven children, without
chastisement, less or more, as the nature and circumstances of the offence require.

"I insist upon conquering the will of children betimes,
because this is the only strong and rational foundation
of a religious education; without which both precept
and example will be ineffectual. But when this is
thoroughly done, then a child is capable of being
governed by the reason and piety of its parents, till its
own understanding comes to maturity, and the principles
of religion have taken root in the mind.

"I cannot yet dismiss this subject. As self-will is
the root of all sin and misery, so whatever cherishes this
in children insures their after-wretchedness and irreligion;
whatever checks and mortifies it promotes their future
happiness and piety. This is still more evident, if we
farther consider, that religion is nothing else than the
doing the will of God, and not our own: that the one
grand impediment to our temporal and eternal happiness
being this self-will, no indulgences of it can be
trivial, no denial unprofitable. Heaven or hell depends

on this alone. So that the parent who studies to subdue it in his child, works together with God in the renewing and saving a soul. The parent who indulges it does the devil's work, makes religion impracticable, salvation unattainable; and does all that in him lies to damn his child, soul and body for ever.

They had Nothing they Cried For

" The children of this family were taught, as soon as they could speak, the Lord's prayer, which they were made to say at rising and bed-time constantly; to which, as they grew bigger, were added a short prayer for their parents, and some collects; a short catechism, and some portion of Scripture, as their memories could bear.

" They were very early made to distinguish the Sabbath from other days; before they could well speak or go. They were as soon taught to be still at family prayers, and to ask a blessing immediately after, which they used to do by signs, before they could kneel or speak.

" They were quickly made to understand they might have nothing they cried for, and instructed to speak handsomely for what they wanted. They were not suffered to ask even the lowest servant for aught without saying, ' Pray give me such a thing '; and the servant was chid, if she ever let them omit that word. Taking God's name in vain, cursing and swearing, profaneness, obscenity, rude, ill-bred names, were never heard among them. Nor were they ever permitted to call each other by their proper names without the addition of brother or sister.

" None of them were taught to read till five years old, except Kezzy, in whose case I was overruled; and she was more years learning than any of the rest had been months. The way of teaching was this: The day

G

before a child began to learn, the house was set in order,
every one's work appointed them, and a charge given
that none should come into the room from nine till
twelve, or from two till five; which, you know, were
our school hours. One day was allowed the child
wherein to learn its letters ; and each of them did in that
time know all its letters, great and small, except Molly
and Nancy, who were a day and a half before they knew
them perfectly ; for which I then thought them very dull ;
but since I have observed how long many children are
learning the horn-book, I have changed my opinion.

"But the reason why I thought them so then was,
because the rest learned so readily ; and your brother
Samuel, who was the first child I ever taught, learned
the alphabet in a few hours. He was five years old on
February 10 ; the next day he began to learn, and as
soon as he knew the letters, began at the first chapter of
Genesis. He was taught to spell the first verse, then to
read it over and over, till he could read it offhand without any hesitation, so on to the second, &c., till he took
ten verses for a lesson, which he quickly did. Easter
fell low that year, and by Whitsuntide he could read a
chapter very well; for he read continually, and had such
a prodigious memory, that I cannot remember ever to
have told him the same word twice.

Keeping the Wesley Children in Order

"What was yet stranger, any word he had learned in
his lesson, he knew, wherever he saw it, either in his
Bible, or any other book ; by which means he learned
very soon to read an English author well.

"The same method was observed with them all. As
soon as they knew the letters, they were put first to spell,
and read one line, then a verse ; never leaving till

perfect in their lesson, were it shorter or longer. So one or other continued reading at school-time, without any intermission; and before we left school, each child read what he had learned that morning; and ere we parted in the afternoon, what they had learned that day.

" There was no such thing as loud talking or playing allowed of; but every one was kept close to their business, for the six hours of school: and it is almost incredible, what a child may be taught in a quarter of a year, by a vigorous application, if it have but a tolerable capacity, and good health. Every one of these, Kezzy excepted, could read better in that time, than the most of women can do as long as they live.

" Rising out of their places, or going out of the room, was not permitted, unless for good cause; and running into the yard, garden, or street, without leave, was always esteemed a capital offence.

" For some years we went on very well. Never were children in better order. Never were children better disposed to piety, or in more subjection to their parents; till that fatal dispersion of them, after the fire, into several families. In those they were left at full liberty to converse with servants, which before they had always been restrained from; and to run abroad, and play with any children, good or bad. They soon learned to neglect a strict observation of the Sabbath, and got knowledge of several songs and bad things, which before they had no notion of. The civil behaviour which made them admired, when at home, by all which saw them, was, in great measure, lost; and a clownish accent, and many rude ways, were learned, which were not reformed without some difficulty.

" When the house was rebuilt, and the children all brought home, we entered upon a strict reform; and then was begun the custom of singing psalms at beginning and leaving school, morning and evening. Then also that of a general retirement at five o'clock was entered upon; when the oldest took the youngest that could speak, and the second the next, to whom they read the Psalms for the day, and a chapter in the New Testament; as, in the morning, they were directed to read the Psalms and a chapter in the Old: after which they went to their private prayers, before they got their breakfast, or came into the family. And, I thank God, the custom is still preserved among us.

Susanna Wesley's "By-laws"

"There were several by-laws observed among us, which slipped my memory, or else they had been inserted in their proper place; but I mention them here, because I think them useful.

"1. It had been observe that cowardice and fear of punishment often lead children into lying, till they get a custom of it, which they cannot leave. To prevent this, a law was made, That whoever was charged with a fault, of which they were guilty, if they would ingenuously confess it, and promise to amend, should not be beaten. This rule prevented a great deal of lying, and would have done more, if one in the family would have observed it. But he could not be prevailed on, and therefore was often imposed on by false colours and equivocations; which none would have used (except one), had they been kindly dealt with. And some, in spite of all, would always speak truth plainly.

"2. That no sinful action, as lying, pilfering, playing at church, or on the Lord's day, disobedience, quarrelling, &c., should ever pass unpunished.

"3. That no child should ever be chid, or beat twice,

for the same fault; and that if they amended, they should never be upbraided with it afterwards.

" 4. That every signal act of obedience, especially when it crossed upon their own inclinations, should be always commended, and frequently rewarded, according to the merits of the cause.

" 5. That if ever any child performed an act of obedience, or did anything with an intention to please, though the performance was not well, yet the obedience and intention should be kindly accepted; and the child with sweetness directed how to do better for the future.

" 6. That propriety be inviolably preserved, and none suffered to invade the property of another in the smallest matter, though it were but of the value of a farthing, or a pin; which they might not take from the owner without, much less against, his consent. This rule can never be too much inculcated on the minds of children; and from the want of parents or governors doing it as they ought, proceeds that shameful neglect of justice which we may observe in the world.

" 7. That promises be strictly observed; and a gift once bestowed, and so the right passed away from the donor, be not resumed, but left to the disposal of him to whom it was given; unless it were conditional, and the condition of the obligation not performed.

" 8. That no girl be taught to work till she can read very well; and then that she be kept to her work with the same application, and for the same time, that she was held to in reading. This rule also is much to be observed; for the putting children to learn sewing before they can read perfectly, is the very reason why so few women can read fit to be heard, and never to be well understood."

Wed. December 1 (Newcastle).—We had several places

offered, on which to build a room for the society; but none was such as we wanted. And perhaps there was a providence in our not finding any as yet; for, by this means, I was kept at Newcastle, whether I would or no.

Sat. 4.—I was both surprised and grieved at a genuine instance of enthusiasm. J—— B——, of Tunfield Leigh, who had received a sense of the love of God a few days before, came riding through the town, hallooing and shouting, and driving all the people before him; telling them, God had told him he should be a king, and should tread all his enemies under his feet. I sent him home immediately to his work, and advised him to cry day and night to God, that he might be lowly in heart; lest Satan should again get an advantage over him.

Mr. Stephenson and Wesley

To-day a gentleman called and offered me a piece of ground. On Monday an article was drawn, wherein he agreed to put me into possession on Thursday, upon payment of thirty pounds.

Tues, 7.—I was so ill in the morning, that I was obliged to send Mr. Williams to the room. He afterwards went to Mr. Stephenson, a merchant in the town, who had a passage through the ground we intended to buy. I was willing to purchase it. Mr. Stephenson told him, "Sir, I do not want money; but if Mr. Wesley wants ground, he may have a piece of my garden, adjoining to the place you mention. I am at a word. For forty pounds he shall have sixteen yards in breadth, and thirty in length."

Wed. 8.—Mr. Stephenson and I signed an article, and I took possession of the ground. But I could not fairly go back from my agreement with Mr. Riddel: so I entered on his ground at the same time. The whole is about forty yards in length; in the middle of which we determined to build the house, leaving room for a small courtyard before, and a little garden behind, the building.

Mon. 13.—I removed into a lodging, adjoining to the ground where we were preparing to build; but the violent frost obliged us to delay the work. I never felt so intense cold before. In a room where a constant fire was kept, though my desk was fixed within a yard of the chimney, I could not write for a quarter of an hour together, without my hands being quite benumbed.

Newcastle's First Methodist Room

Mon. 20.—We laid the first stone of the house. Many were gathered, from all parts, to see it; but none scoffed or interrupted while we praised God, and prayed that He would prosper the work of our hands upon us. Three or four times in the evening, I was forced to break off preaching, that we might pray and give thanks to God.

Thur. 23.—It being computed that such a house as was proposed could not be finished under £700, many were positive it would never be finished at all; others, that I should not live to see it covered. I was of another mind; nothing doubting but, as it was begun for God's sake, He would provide what was needful for the finishing it.

1743. Sat. January 1.—Between Doncaster and Epworth I overtook one who immediately accosted me with so many and so impertinent questions, that I was quite amazed. In the midst of some of them, concerning my travels and my journey, I interrupted him, and asked, "Are you aware that we are on a longer journey; that we are travelling toward eternity?" He replied instantly,

"O, I find you! I find you! I know where you are! Is not your name Wesley? 'Tis pity! 'Tis great pity! Why could not your father's religion serve you? Why must you have a new religion?" I was going to reply; but he cut me short by crying out in triumph, "I am a Christian! I am a Christian! I am a Churchman! I am a Churchman! I am none of your Culamites"; as plain as he could speak; for he was so drunk, he could but just keep his seat. Having then clearly won the day, or, as his phrase was, "put them all down," he began kicking his horse on both sides and rode off as fast as he could.

Wesley Refused the Sacrament at Epworth

In the evening I reached Epworth. Sunday, 2. At five I preached on, "So is every one that is born of the Spirit." About eight I preached from my father's tomb on Heb. viii. 11. Many from the neighbouring towns asked, if it would not be well, as it was sacrament Sunday, for them to receive it. I told them, "By all means: but it would be more respectful first to ask Mr. Romley, the curate's leave." One did so, in the name of the rest; to whom he said, "Pray tell Mr. Wesley, I shall not give him the sacrament; for he is not fit."

How wise a God is our God! There could not have been so fit a place under heaven, where this should befall me first as my father's house, the place of my nativity, and the very place where, "according to the straitest sect of our religion," I had so long "lived a Pharisee!" It was also fit, in the highest degree, that he who repelled me from that very table, where I had myself so often distributed the bread of life, should be one who owed his all in this world to the tender love which my father had shown to his, as well as personally to himself.

Tues. 22.—I went to South-Biddick, a village of colliers seven miles south-east of Newcastle. The spot where I stood was just at the bottom of a semi-circular hill, on the rising sides of which many hundreds stood; but far more on the plain beneath. I cried to them, in the words of the prophet, "O ye dry bones, hear the word of the Lord!" Deep attention sat on every face; so that here also I believed it would be well to preach weekly.

Wesley and the Cock-fighter

Wed. 23.—I met a gentleman in the streets cursing and swearing in so dreadful a manner, that I could not but stop him. He soon grew calmer; told me he must treat me with a glass of wine; and that he would come and hear me, only he was afraid I should say something against fighting of cocks.

April 1. (Being Good Friday.)—I had a great desire to visit a little village called Placey, about ten measured miles north of Newcastle. It is inhabited by colliers only, and such as had been always in the first rank for savage ignorance and wickedness of every kind. Their grand assembly used to be on the Lord's day; on which men, women, and children met together to dance, fight, curse and swear, and play at chuck ball, span-farthing, or whatever came next to hand. I felt great compassion for these poor creatures, from the time I heard of them first; and the more, because all men seemed to despair of them.

Between seven and eight I set out with John Heally, my guide. The north wind, being unusually high, drove the sleet in our face, which froze as it fell, and cased us over presently. When we came to Placey, we could very hardly stand. As soon as we were a little

recovered I went into the square, and declared Him who
"was wounded for our transgressions" and "bruised
for our iniquities." The poor sinners were quickly
gathered together and gave earnest heed to the things
which were spoken. And so they did in the afternoon
again, in spite of the wind and snow, when I besought
them to receive Him for their King; to "repent and
believe the Gospel."

Wesley in Seven Dials

Sun. May 29.—I began officiating at the chapel
in West Street, near the Seven Dials, of which (by a
strange chain of providences) we have a lease for several
years. I preached on the Gospel for the day, part of
the third chapter of St. John; and afterwards administered the Lord's Supper to some hundreds of communicants. I was a little afraid at first, that my strength
would not suffice for the business of the day, when a
service of five hours (for it lasted from ten to three) was
added to my usual employment. But God looked to
that: so I must think; and they that will call it
enthusiasm may. I preached at the Great-gardens at
five to an immense congregation, on, "Ye must be born
again." Then the leaders met (who filled all the time
that I was not speaking in public); and after them, the
bands. At ten at night I was less weary than at six in
the morning.

Sun. July 10 (Newcastle).—I preached at eight on
Chowden Fell, on, "Why will ye die, O house of Israel?"
Ever since I came to Newcastle the first time, my spirit
had been moved within me, at the crowds of poor
wretches, who were every Sunday, in the afternoon
sauntering to and fro on the Sandhill. I resolved, if
possible, to find them a better employ; and as soon as

the service at All Saints was over, walked straight from
the church to the Sandhill, and gave out a verse of a
psalm. In a few minutes I had company enough;
thousands upon thousands crowding together. But the
prince of this world fought with all his might lest his
kingdom should be overthrown. Indeed, the very mob
of Newcastle, in the height of their rudeness, have
commonly some humanity left. I scarce observed that
they threw any thing at all; neither did I receive the
least personal hurt: but they continued thrusting one
another to and fro, and making such a noise, that my
voice could not be heard: so that, after spending near
an hour in singing and prayer, I thought it best to
adjourn to our own house.

Wesley's Horses give Trouble

Mon. 18.—I set out from Newcastle with John
Downes, of Horsley. We were four hours riding to
Ferry Hill, about twenty measured miles. After resting
there an hour we rode softly on; and, at two o'clock,
came to Darlington. I thought my horse was not well;
he thought the same of his; though they were both
young, and very well the day before. We ordered the
hostler to fetch a farrier, which he did without delay;
but, before the men could determine what was the
matter, both the horses lay down and died.

I hired a horse to Sandhutton, and rode on, desiring
John Downes to follow me. Thence I rode to Borough-
bridge on Tuesday morning, and then walked on to
Leeds.

Mon. August 22 (London).—After a few of us had
joined in prayer, about four I set out and rode softly to
Snow Hill; where, the saddle slipping quite upon my
mare's neck, I fell over her head, and she ran back into

Smithfield. Some boys caught her and brought her to me again, cursing and swearing all the way. I spoke plainly to them, and they promised to amend. I was setting forward, when a man cried, "Sir, you have lost your saddle-cloth." Two or three more would needs help me to put it on; but these, too, swore at almost every word. I turned to one and another, and spoke in love. They all took it well, and thanked me much. I gave them two or three little books, which they promised to read over carefully.

Before I reached Kensington, I found my mare had lost a shoe. This gave me an opportunity of talking closely, for near half an hour, both to the smith and his servant. I mention these little circumstances to show how easy it is to redeem every fragment of time (if I may so speak), when we feel any love to those souls for which Christ died.

Wesley Goes to Cornwall

Fri. 26.—I set out for Cornwall. In the evening I preached at the cross in Taunton, on, "The kingdom of God is not meat and drink; but righteousness, and peace, and joy in the Holy Ghost." A poor man had posted himself behind, in order to make some disturbance: but the time was not come; the zealous wretches who "deny the Lord that bought them" had not yet stirred up the people. Many cried out, "Throw down that rascal there; knock him down; beat out his brains": so that I was obliged to entreat for him more than once, or he would have been but roughly handled.

Sat. 27.—I reached Exeter in the afternoon; but as no one knew of my coming, I did not preach that night, only to one poor sinner at the inn; who, after listening to our conversation for a while, looked earnestly at us, and asked, whether it was possible for one, who had in some measure known " the power of the world to come," and was " fallen away " (which she said was her case), to be " renewed again to repentance." We besought God in her behalf, and left her sorrowing; and yet not without hope.

Sun. 28.—I preached at seven to a handful of people. The sermon we heard at church was quite innocent of meaning: what that in the afternoon was, I know not; for I could not hear a single sentence.

From church I went to the castle; where were gathered together (as some imagined) half the grown persons in the city. It was an awful sight. So vast a congregation in that solemn amphitheatre! And all silent and still, while I explained at large, and enforced, that glorious truth, " Happy are they whose iniquities are forgiven, and whose sins are covered."

Mon. 29.—We rode forward. About sunset we were in the middle of the first great pathless moor beyond Launceston. About eight we were got quite out of the way; but we had not got far before we heard Bodmin bell. Directed by this we turned to the left and came to the town before nine.

Tues. 30.—In the evening we reached St. Ives. At seven I invited all guilty, helpless sinners, who were conscious they " had nothing to pay," to accept of free forgiveness. The room was crowded both within and without; but all were quiet and attentive.

Wed. 31.—I spoke severally with those of the society, who were about one hundred and twenty. Near an hundred of these had found peace with God: such is the blessing of being persecuted for righteousness' sake ! As we were going to church at eleven, a large company at the market-place welcomed us with a loud huzza:

wit as harmless as the ditty sung under my window (composed, one assured me, by a gentlewoman of their own town),

> " Charles Wesley is come to town,
>   To try if he can pull the churches down."

In the evening I explained "the promise of the Father." After preaching, many began to be turbulent; but John Nelson went into the midst of them, spoke a little to the loudest, who answered not again, but went quietly away.

The Cornish Tinners

Sat. September 3.—I rode to the Three-cornered Down (so called), nine or ten miles east of St. Ives, where we found two or three hundred tinners, who had been some time waiting for us. They all appeared quite pleased and unconcerned; and many of them ran after us to Gwennap (two miles east), where their number was quickly increased to four or five hundred. I had much comfort here, in applying these words, "He hath anointed me to preach the Gospel to the poor." One who lived near invited us to lodge at his house, and conducted us back to the Green in the morning. We came thither just as the day dawned.

I strongly applied those gracious words, "I will heal their backslidings, I will love them freely," to five or six hundred serious people. At Trezuthan Downs, five miles nearer St. Ives, we found seven or eight hundred people, to whom I cried aloud, "Cast away all your transgressions; for why will ye die, O house of Israel?" After dinner I preached again to about a thousand people, on Him whom "God hath exalted to be a Prince and a Saviour." It was here first I observed a little impression made on two or three of the hearers; the rest, as usual, showing huge approbation, and absolute unconcern.

Fri. 9.—I rode in quest of St. Hilary Downs, ten or twelve miles south-east of St. Ives. And the Downs I found, but no congregation—neither man, woman, nor child. But by that I had put on my gown and cassock, about an hundred gathered themselves together, whom I earnestly called "to repent and believe the Gospel." And if but one heard, it was worth all the labour.

Sat. 10.—There were prayers at St. Just in the afternoon, which did not end till four. I then preached at the Cross, to, I believe, a thousand people, who all behaved in a quiet and serious manner.

At six I preached at Sennan, near the Land's End; and appointed the little congregation (consisting chiefly of old, grey-headed men) to meet me again at five in the morning. But on Sunday, 11, great part of them were got together between three and four o'clock: so between four and five we began praising God; and I largely explained and applied, "I will heal their backslidings; I will love them freely."

We went afterwards down, as far as we could go safely, toward the point of the rocks at the Land's End. It was an awful sight! But how will these melt away, when God shall arise to judgment! The sea between does indeed "boil like a pot." "One would think the deep to be hoary." But "though they swell, yet can they not prevail. He hath set their bounds, which they cannot pass."

Between eight and nine I preached at St. Just, on the green plain near the town, to the largest congregation (I was informed) that ever had been seen in these parts. I cried out, with all the authority of love, "Why will ye die, O house of Israel?" The people trembled, and

were still. I had not known such an hour before in
Cornwall.

In the Scilly Isles

Mon. 12.—I had had for some time a great desire to
go and publish the love of God our Saviour, if it were
but for one day, in the Isles of Scilly; and I had occasionally mentioned it to several. This evening three of
our brethren came and offered to carry me thither, if I
could procure the mayor's boat, which, they said, was
the best sailer of any in the town. I sent, and he lent
it me immediately. So the next morning, Tuesday, 13,
John Nelson, Mr. Shepherd, and I, with three men and
a pilot, sailed from St. Ives. It seemed strange to me to
attempt going in a fisher-boat, fifteen leagues upon the
main ocean; especially when the waves began to swell,
and hang over our heads. But I called to my companions, and we all joined together in singing lustily and
with a good courage :

> "When passing through the watery deep,
>   I ask in faith his promised aid ;
> The waves an awful distance keep,
>   And shrink from my devoted head;
> Fearless their violence I dare :
> They cannot harm—for God is there."

About half an hour after one, we landed on St. Mary's,
the chief of the inhabited islands.

We immediately waited upon the Governor, with the
usual present, viz., a newspaper. I desired him, likewise,
to accept of an "Earnest Appeal." The minister not
being willing I should preach in the church, I preached,
at six, in the streets, to almost all the town, and many
soldiers, sailors, and workmen, on, "Why will ye die, O
house of Israel?" It was a blessed time, so that I
scarce knew how to conclude. After sermon I gave

them some little books and hymns, which they were so
eager to receive, that they were ready to tear both them
and me to pieces.

For what political reason such a number of workmen
were gathered together, and employed at so large an
expense, to fortify a few barren rocks, which whosoever
would take, deserves to have them for his pains, I could
not possibly devise: but a providential reason was easy
to be discovered. God might call them together to hear
the Gospel, which perhaps otherwise they might never
have thought of.

At five in the morning I preached again, on, "I will
heal their backslidings; I will love them freely." And
between nine and ten, having talked with many in private,
and distributed both to them and others between two and
three hundred hymns and little books, we left this barren,
dreary place, and set sail for St. Ives, though the wind
was strong, and blew directly in our teeth. Our pilot
said we should have good luck if we reached the land ;
but he knew not Him whom the winds and seas obey.
Soon after three we were even with the Land's End, and
about nine we reached St. Ives.

Remarkable Service at Gwennap

Tues. 20.—At Trezuthan Downs I preached to two or
three thousand people, on the "highway" of the Lord,
the way of holiness. We reached Gwennap a little
before six, and found the plain covered from end to end.
It was supposed there were ten thousand people; to
whom I preached Christ our "wisdom, righteousness,
sanctification, and redemption." I could not conclude
till it was so dark we could scarce see one another. And
there was on all sides the deepest attention ; none speaking, stirring, or scarce looking aside. Surely here, though

H

in a temple not made with hands, was God worshipped
in "the beauty of holiness."

Wed. 21.—I was waked between three and four, by a
large company of tinners, who, fearing they should be
too late, had gathered round the house, and were singing and praising God. At five I preached once more,
on, "Believe on the Lord Jesus Christ, and thou shalt
be saved." They all devoured the word. O may it be
health to their soul, and marrow unto their bones!

We rode to Launceston that day. Thursday, 22. As
we were riding through a village called Sticklepath, one
stopped me in the street, and asked abruptly, "Is not
thy name John Wesley?" Immediately two or three
more came up, and told me I must stop there. I did
so; and before we had spoke many words, our souls
took acquaintance with each other. I found they were
called Quakers: but that hurt not me; seeing the love
of God was in their hearts.

A Mob at Wednesbury

Thur. Oct. 20.—After preaching to a small, attentive
congregation (at Birmingham), I rode to Wednesbury.
At twelve I preached in a ground near the middle of
the town, to a far larger congregation than was expected,
on, "Jesus Christ, the same yesterday, and to-day, and
for ever." I believe every one present felt the power of
God: and no creature offered to molest us, either going
or coming; but the Lord fought for us, and we held our
peace.

I was writing at Francis Ward's, in the afternoon, when
the cry arose, that the mob had beset the house. We
prayed that God would disperse them; and it was so:
one went this way, and another that; so that, in half an
hour, not a man was left. I told our brethren, "Now

is the time for us to go "; but they pressed me exceedingly
to stay. So, that I might not offend them, I sat down,
though I foresaw what would follow. Before five the mob
surrounded the house again, in greater numbers than
ever. The cry of one and all was, "Bring out the
minister; we will have the minister."

I desired one to take their captain by the hand, and
bring him into the house. After a few sentences inter-
changed between us, the lion was become a lamb. I
desired him to go and bring one or two more of the most
angry of his companions. He brought in two, who were
ready to swallow the ground with rage; but in two
minutes they were as calm as he. I then bade them
make way, that I might go out among the people.

As soon as I was in the midst of them, I called
for a chair; and standing up, asked, "What do any of
you want with me?" Some said, "We want you to go
with us to the justice." I replied, "That I will, with
all my heart." I then spoke a few words, which God
applied; so that they cried out, with might and main,
"The gentleman is an honest gentleman, and we will
spill our blood in his defence." I asked, "Shall we go
to the justice to-night, or in the morning?" Most
of them cried, "To-night, to-night"; on which I went
before, and two or three hundred followed; the rest
returning whence they came.

The night came on before we had walked a mile,
together with heavy rain. However, on we went to
Bentley Hall, two miles from Wednesbury. One or two
ran before, to tell Mr. Lane they had brought Mr.
Wesley before his worship.   Mr. Lane replied, "What
nave I to do with Mr. Wesley? Go and carry him back
again." By this time the main body came up, and began
knocking at the door. A servant told them Mr. Lane

was in bed. His son followed, and asked what was the matter. One replied, " Why, an't please you, they sing psalms all day; nay, and make folks rise at five in the morning. And what would your worship advise us to do?" "To go home," said Mr. Lane, "and be quiet."

Wesley in Danger

Here they were all at a full stop, till one advised, to go to Justice Persehouse, at Walsal. All agreed to this; so we hastened on, and about seven came to his house. But Mr. P—— likewise sent word, that he was in bed. Now they were at a stand again; but at last they all thought it the wisest course to make the best of their way home. About fifty of them undertook to convoy me. But we had not gone a hundred yards, when the mob of Walsal came, pouring in like a flood, and bore down all before them. The Darlaston mob made what defence they could; but they were weary, as well as out-numbered: so that in a short time, many being knocked down, the rest ran away, and left me in their hands.

To attempt speaking was vain; for the noise on every side was like the roaring of the sea. So they dragged me along till we came to the town; where seeing the door of a large house open, I attempted to go in; but a man, catching me by the hair, pulled me back into the middle of the mob. They made no more stop till they had carried me through the main street, from one end of the town to the other. I continued speaking all the time to those within hearing, feeling no pain or weariness. At the west end of the town, seeing a door half open, I made toward it, and would have gone in; but a gentleman in the shop would not suffer me, saying, they would pull the house down to the ground. However, I stood at the door, and asked, "Are you willing to hear me

speak?" Many cried out, "No, no! knock his brains
out; down with him; kill him at once." Others said,
"Nay, but we will hear him first." I began asking,
"What evil have I done? Which of you all have I
wronged in word or deed?" And continued speaking
for above a quarter of an hour, till my voice suddenly
failed: then the floods began to lift up their voice
again; many crying out, "Bring him away! bring him
away!"

In the mean time my strength and my voice returned,
and I broke out aloud in prayer. And now the man
who just before headed the mob, turned, and said, "Sir,
I will spend my life for you: follow me, and not one
soul here shall touch a hair of your head." Two or
three of his fellows confirmed his words, and got close
to me immediately. At the same time, the gentleman
in the shop cried out, "For shame, for shame! Let
him go."

An honest butcher, who was a little farther off, said it
was a shame they should do thus; and pulled back four
or five, one after another, who were running on the most
fiercely. The people then, as if it had been by common
consent, fell back to the right and left; while those three
or four men took me between them, and carried me
through them all. But on the bridge the mob rallied
again: we therefore went on one side, over the mill-dam,
and thence through the meadows; till, a little before
ten, God brought me safe to Wednesbury; having lost
only one flap of my waistcoat, and a little skin from one
of my hands.

His Presence of Mind

I never saw such a chain of providences before; so
many convincing proofs, that the hand of God is on

every person and thing, and overruling all as it seemeth Him good.

The poor woman of Darlaston, who had headed that mob, and sworn, that no one should touch me, when she saw her followers give way, ran into the thickest of the throng, and knocked down three or four men, one after another. But many assaulting her at once, she was soon overpowered, and had probably been killed in a few minutes (three men keeping her down and beating her with all their might), had not a man called to one of them, " Hold, Tom, hold ! " " Who is there ? " said Tom : " what, honest Munchin ? Nay, then, let her go." So they held their hand, and let her get up and crawl home as well as she could.

From the beginning to the end I found the same presence of mind, as if I had been sitting in my own study. But I took no thought for one moment before another; only once it came into my mind, that if they should throw me into the river, it would spoil the papers that were in my pocket. For myself, I did not doubt but I should swim across, having but a thin coat, and a light pair of boots.

The circumstances that follow, I thought, were particularly remarkable : 1. That many endeavoured to throw me down while we were going down-hill on a slippery path to the town ; as well judging, that if I was once on the ground, I should hardly rise any more. But I made no stumble at all, nor the least slip till I was entirely out of their hands. 2. That although many strove to lay hold on my collar or clothes, to pull me down, they could not fasten at all : only one got fast hold of the flap of my waistcoat, which was soon left in his hand ; the other flap, in the pocket of which was a bank note, was torn but half off. 3. That a lusty man just behind struck at me several times, with a large oaken stick; with which if he had struck me once on the back part of my head, it would have saved him all farther trouble. But every time the blow was turned aside, I know not how; for I could not move to the right hand or left.

"What Soft Hair He Has"

4. That another came rushing through the press, and raising his arm to strike, on a sudden let it drop, and only stroked my head, saying, " What soft hair he has ! " 5. That I stopped exactly at the mayor's door, as if I had known it (which the mob doubtless thought I did), and found him standing in the shop, which gave the first check to the madness of the people. 6. That the very first men whose hearts were turned were the heroes of the town, the captains of the rabble on all occasions, one of them having been a prize-fighter at the bear-garden.

7. That from first to last, I heard none give a reviling word, or call me by any opprobrious name what-ever; but the cry of one and all was: " The Preacher ! The Preacher ! The Parson ! The Minister ! " 8. That no creature, at least within my hearing, laid anything to my charge, either true or false; having in the hurry quite forgot to provide themselves with an accusation of any kind. And, lastly, that they were as utterly at a loss, what they should do with me; none proposing any determinate thing; only, " Away with him ! Kill him at once ! "

By how gentle degrees does God prepare us for his will ! Two years ago a piece of brick grazed my shoulders. It was a year after that the stone struck me between the eyes. Last month I received one blow, and this evening two; one before we came into the town, and one after we were gone out ; but both were as nothing : for though one man struck me on the breast with all his might, and the other on the mouth with such a force that the blood gushed out immediately, I felt no more pain from either of the blows, than if they had touched me with a straw.

It ought not to be forgotten, that when the rest of the society made all haste to escape for their lives, four only would not stir, William Sitch, Edward Slater, John Griffiths, and Joan Parks : these kept with me, resolving to live or die together ; and none of them received one blow, but William Sitch, who held me by the arm, from one end of the town to the other. He was then dragged away and knocked down ; but he soon rose and got to me again. I afterwards asked him, what he expected when the mob came upon us ? He said, " To die for Him who had died for us " : and he felt no hurry or fear ; but calmly waited till God should require his soul of him.

Wesley's Defenders

I asked J. Parks, if she was not afraid when they tore her from me ? She said, " No ; no more than I am now. I could trust God for you, as well as for myself. From the beginning I had a full persuasion that God would deliver you. I knew not how ; but I left that to Him, and was as sure as if it were already done." I asked, if the report was true that she had fought for me. She said, " No ; I knew God would fight for His children." And shall these souls perish at the last ?

When I came back to Francis Ward's I found many of our brethren waiting upon God. Many also whom I never had seen before came to rejoice with us. And the next morning, as I rode through the town in my way to Nottingham, every one I met expressed such a cordial affection, that I could scarce believe what I saw and heard.

The Sleepy Magistrates' Proclamation

I cannot close this head without inserting as great a curiosity in its kind as, I believe, was ever yet seen in England; which had its birth within a very few days of this remarkable occurrence at Walsal.

"*Staffordshire.*

" To all High-Constables, Petty-Constables, and other of his Majesty's Peace Officers, within the said County, and particularly to the Constable of Tipton " (near Walsal) :

"WHEREAS, we, his Majesty's Justices of the Peace for the said County of Stafford, have received information that several disorderly persons, styling themselves Methodist Preachers, go about raising routs and riots, to the great damage of his Majesty's liege people, and against the peace of our Sovereign Lord the King :

" These are, in his Majesty's name, to command you and every one of you, within your respective districts, to make diligent search after the said Methodist Preachers, and to bring him or them before some of us his said Majesty's Justices of the Peace, to be examined concerning their unlawful doings.

" Given under our hands and seals, this   day of October, 1743.

"J. LANE.
" W. PERSEHOUSE.

N.B.—The very justices to whose houses I was carried, and who severally refused to see me !

Sat. 22.—I rode from Nottingham to Epworth, and on Monday set out for Grimsby: but at Ferry we were at a full stop, the boatmen telling us we could not pass the Trent; it was as much as our lives were worth to put from shore before the storm abated. We waited an hour; but, being afraid it would do much hurt, if I should disappoint the congregation at Grimsby, I asked the men if they did not think it possible to get to the other shore: they said, they could not tell; but if we would venture our lives, they would venture theirs. So we put off, having six men, two women, and three horses, in the boat.

Wesley Nearly Drowned

Many stood looking after us on the river-side, in the middle of which we were, when, in an instant, the side of the boat was under water, and the horses and men rolling one over another. We expected the boat to sink every moment; but I did not doubt of being able to swim ashore. The boatmen were amazed as well as the rest; but they quickly recovered and rowed for life. And soon after, our horses leaping overboard, lightened the boat, and we all came unhurt to land.

They wondered what was the matter I did not rise (for I lay along in the bottom of the boat), and I wondered too, till, upon examination, I found that a large iron crow, which the boatmen sometimes used, was (none knew how) run through the string of my boot, which pinned me down that I could not stir; so that if the boat had sunk, I should have been safe enough from swimming any further.

The same day, and, as near as we could judge, the same hour, the boat in which my brother was crossing the Severn, at the New Passage, was carried away by

the wind, and in the utmost danger of splitting upon
the rocks. But the same God, when all human hope
was past, delivered them as well as us.

Methodism on the Stage

Mon. 31.—We set out early in the morning, and in
the evening came to Newcastle.

Wed. November 2.—The following advertisement was
published :

FOR THE BENEFIT OF MR. ESTE.

By the Edinburgh Company of Comedians, on Friday, November 4,
will be acted a Comedy, called,

THE CONSCIOUS LOVERS;

To which will be added a Farce, called,

TRICK UPON TRICK, or METHODISM DISPLAYED

On Friday, a vast multitude of spectators were assembled in the Moot Hall to see this. It was believed
there could not be less than fifteen hundred people,
some hundreds of whom sat on rows of seats built upon
the stage. Soon after the comedians had begun the
first act of the play, on a sudden all those seats fell
down at once, the supporters of them breaking like a
rotten stick. The people were thrown one upon another,
about five foot forward, but not one of them hurt.
After a short time the rest of the spectators were quiet,
and the actors went on. In the middle of the second
act, all the shilling seats gave a crack, and sunk several
inches down. A great noise and shrieking followed ;
and as many as could readily get to the door, went out,
and returned no more. Notwithstanding this, when the
noise was over, the actors went on with the play.

In the beginning of the third act the entire stage
suddenly sunk about six inches : the players retired

with great precipitation; yet in a while they began
again. At the latter end of the third act, all the
sixpenny seats, without any kind of notice, fell to the
ground. There was now a cry on every side; it
being supposed that many were crushed in pieces: but,
upon inquiry, not a single person (such was the mercy
of God!) was either killed or dangerously hurt. Two or
three hundred remaining still in the hall, Mr. Este (who
was to act the Methodist) came upon the stage and told
them, for all this he was resolved the farce should be
acted. While he was speaking, the stage sunk six
inches more; on which he ran back in the utmost
confusion, and the people as fast as they could out of
the door, none staying to look behind him.

Which is most surprising—that those players acted
this farce the next week—or that some hundreds of
people came again to see it?

The First Conference

1744. Mon. June 18.—I left Epworth; and on
Wednesday, 20, in the afternoon, met my brother in
London.

Monday, 25, and the five following days, we spent in
conference with many of our brethren (come from several
parts), who desire nothing but to save their own souls,
and those who hear them. And surely, as long as they
continue thus minded, their labour shall not be in vain
in the Lord.

The next day we endeavoured to purge the society of
all that did not walk according to the Gospel. By this
means we reduced the number of members to less than
nineteen hundred. But number is an inconsiderable
circumstance. May God increase them in faith and
love!

Fri. Aug. 24.—(St. Bartholomew's day.) I preached, I suppose the last time, at St. Mary's [Oxford]. Be it so. I am now clear of the blood of these men. I have fully delivered my own soul.

The Beadle came to me afterwards, and told me the Vice-Chancellor had sent him for my notes. I sent them without delay, not without admiring the wise providence of God. Perhaps few men of note would have given a sermon of mine the reading, if I had put t into their hands; but by this means it came to be read, probably more than once, by every man of eminence in the University.

Wesley's Chancery Bill

Thur. Dec. 27.—I called on the solicitor whom I had employed in the suit lately commenced in Chancery; and here I first saw that foul monster, a Chancery bill! A scroll it was of forty-two pages, in large folio, to tell a story which needed not to have taken up forty lines! and stuffed with such stupid senseless, improbable lies (many of them, too, quite foreign to the question) as, I believe, would have cost the compiler his life in any heathen court of either Greece or Rome. And this is equity in a Christian country! This is the English method of redressing other grievances!

1745. Sat. Jan. 5.—I had often wondered at myself (and sometimes mentioned it to others), that ten thousand cares, of various kinds, were no more weight and burden to my mind, than ten thousand hairs were to my head. Perhaps I began to ascribe something of this to my own strength. And thence it might be, that on Sunday, 13, that strength was withheld, and I felt what it was to be troubled about many things. One, and another, hurrying me continually, it seized upon my spirit more and more, till I found it absolutely necessary to fly for my life; and that without delay. So the next day, Monday, 14, I took horse, and rode away for Bristol.

Between Bath and Bristol I was earnestly desired to turn aside, and call at the house of a poor man, William Shalwood. I found him and his wife sick in one bed, and with small hopes of the recovery of either. Yet (after prayer) I believed they would "not die, but live, and declare the loving-kindness of the Lord." The next time I called he was sitting below stairs, and his wife able to go abroad.

As soon as we came into the house at Bristol, my soul was lightened of her load, of that insufferable weight which had lain upon my mind, more or less, for several days. On Sunday, several of our friends from Wales, and other parts, joined with us in the great sacrifice of thanksgiving. And every day we found more and more cause to praise God, and to give him thanks for His still increasing benefits.

Mon. Feb. 18.—I set out with Richard Moss from London for Newcastle.

Wesley's Effective Letter

Sun. March 3.—As I was walking up Pilgrim-street, hearing a man call after me, I stood still. He came up, and used much abusive language, intermixed with many oaths and curses. Several people came out to see what was the matter; on which he pushed me twice or thrice, and went away.

Upon inquiry, I found this man had signalized himself a long season, by abusing and throwing stones at any of our family who went that way. Therefore I would not lose the opportunity, but on Monday, 4, sent him the following note:

" ROBERT YOUNG,—I expect to see you, between this and Friday, and to hear from you, that you are sensible of your fault; otherwise, in pity to your soul, I shall be obliged to inform the magistrates of your assaulting me yesterday in the street.

"I am,

"Your real friend,

"JOHN WESLEY."

Within two or three hours, Robert Young came and promised a quite different behaviour. So did this gentle reproof, if not save a soul from death, yet prevent a multitude of sins.

Sat. April 6.—Mr. Stephenson, of whom I bought the ground on which our house is built, came at length, after delaying it more than two years, and executed the writings. So I am freed from one more care. May I in every thing make known my request to God!

Press Gang and Methodists

Wed. June 19 (Redruth).—Being informed here of what had befallen Mr. Maxfield, we turned aside toward Crowan church-town. But in the way we received information, that he had been removed from thence the night before. It seems, the valiant constables who guarded him, having received timely notice, that a body of five hundred Methodists were coming to take him away by force, had, with great precipitation, carried him two miles further, to the house of one Henry Tomkins.

Here we found him, nothing terrified by his adversaries. I desired Henry Tomkins to show me the warrant. It was directed by Dr. Borlase, and his father, and Mr. Eustick, to the constables and overseers of several parishes, requiring them to " apprehend

all such able-bodied men as had no lawful calling or
sufficient maintenance "; and to bring them before the
aforesaid gentlemen at Marazion, on Friday, 21, to be
examined, whether they were proper persons to serve
his Majesty in the land-service.

It was indorsed, by the steward of Sir John St.
Aubyn, with the names of seven or eight persons, most
of whom were well known to have lawful callings, and a
sufficient maintenance thereby. But that was all one:
they were called " Methodists "; therefore, soldiers they
must be. Underneath was added, "A person, his name
unknown, who disturbs the peace of the parish."

A word to the wise. The good men easily understood, this could be none but the Methodist Preacher;
for who " disturbs the peace of the parish " like one who
tells all drunkards, whoremongers, and common swearers,
" You are in the high road to hell" ?

When we came out of the house, forty or fifty myrmi-
dons stood ready to receive us. But I turned full upon
them, and their courage failed : nor did they recover till
we were at some distance. Then they began blustering
again, and throwing stones; one of which struck Mr.
Thompson's servant.

Fri. 21.—We rode to Marazion. (Vulgarly called
Market-jew.) Finding the justices were not met, we
walked up St. Michael's Mount. The house at the top
is surprisingly large and pleasant. Sir John St. Aubyn
had taken much pains, and been at a considerable expense, in repairing and beautifying the apartments ; and
when the seat was finished, the owner died !

About two, Mr. Thompson and I went into the room
where the justices and commissioners were. After a
few minutes, Dr. Borlase stood up and asked, whether
we had any business. I told him, " We have." We

I never saw before, no, not at Walsal itself, the hand
of God so plainly shown as here. There I had many
companions who were willing to die with me: here, not
a friend, but one simple girl, who likewise was hurried
away from me in an instant, as soon as ever she came
out of Mrs. B.'s door. There I received some blows,
lost part of my clothes, and was covered over with dirt:
here, although the hands of perhaps some hundreds of
people were lifted up to strike or throw, yet they were
one and all stopped in the mid-way; so that not a
man touched me with one of his fingers; neither was
anything thrown from first to last; so that I had not
even a speck of dirt on my clothes. Who can deny
that God heareth the prayer, or that He hath all power
in heaven and earth?

"I Am John Wesley"

I took boat at about half an hour past five. Many
of the mob waited at the end of the town, who, seeing
me escaped out of their hands, could only revenge
themselves with their tongues. But a few of the
fiercest ran along the shore, to receive me at my landing. I walked up the steep narrow passage from the
sea, at the top of which the foremost man stood. I
looked him· in the face, and said, "I wish you a good
night." He spake not, nor moved hand or foot till I
was on horseback. Then he said, "I wish you was in
hell," and turned back to his companions.

As soon as I came within sight of Tolcarn (in
Wendron parish), where I was to preach in the evening,
I was met by many, running as it were for their lives,
and begging me to go no further. I asked, "Why
not?" They said, "The churchwardens and constables, and all the heads of the parish, are waiting

for you at the top of the hill, and are resolved to have you : they have a special warrant from the justices met at Helstone, who will stay there till you are brought." I rode directly up the hill, and observing four or five horsemen, well dressed, went straight to them, and said, " Gentlemen, has any of you anything to say to me ?— I am John Wesley."

One of them appeared extremely angry at this, that I should presume to say I was " Mr. John Wesley." And I know not how I might have fared for advancing so bold an assertion, but that Mr. Collins, the minister of Redruth (accidently, as he said) came by.   Upon his accosting me, and saying he knew me at Oxford, my first antagonist was silent, and a dispute of another kind began : whether this preaching had done any good.   I appealed to matter of fact.   He allowed (after many words), " People are the better for the present " ; but added, " To be sure, by and by they will be as bad, if not worse than ever."

When he rode away, one of the riders said, " Sir, I would speak with you a little ; let us ride to the gate." We did so, and he said, " Sir, I will tell you the ground of this.   All the gentlemen of these parts say, that you have been a long time in France and Spain, and are now sent hither by the Pretender ; and that these societies are to join him."   Nay, surely " all the gentlemen in these parts " will not lie against their own conscience !

I rode hence to a friend's house, some miles off, and found the sleep of a labouring man is sweet.   I was informed there were many here also who had an earnest desire to hear " this preaching," but they did not dare ; Sir —— V——n having solemnly declared, nay, and that in the face of the whole congregation, as they were coming out of church, "If any man of this parish dares hear these fellows, he shall not come to my Christmas-feast !"

Sat. 6.—I rode with Mr. Shepherd to Gwennap. Here also we found the people in the utmost consternation. Word was brought, that a great company of tinners, made drunk on purpose, were coming to do terrible things. I laboured much to compose their minds : but fear had no ears ; so that abundance of people went away. I preached to the rest, on, "Love your enemies." The event showed this also was a false alarm, an artifice of the devil, to hinder men from hearing the word of God.

Wesley Pushed from a High Wall

Sun. 7.—I preached, at five, to a quiet congregation, and about eight, at Stithians. Between six and seven in the evening we came to Tolcarn. Hearing the mob was rising again, I began preaching immediately. I had not spoke a quarter of an hour before they came in view. One Mr. Trounce rode up first, and began speaking to me, wherein he was roughly interrupted by his companions. Yet, as I stood on a high wall, and kept my eyes upon them, many were softened, and grew calmer and calmer ; which some of their champions observing, went round and suddenly pushed me down. I light on my feet, without any hurt ; and finding myself close to the warmest of the horsemen, I took hold of his hand and held it fast, while I expostulated the case. As for being convinced, he was quite above it : however, both he and his fellows grew much milder, and we parted very civilly.

Mon. 8.—I preached at five, on, "Watch and pray," to a quiet and earnest congregation. We then rode on to St. Ives, the most still and honourable post (so are the times changed) which we have in Cornwall.

Tues. 9.—I had just begun preaching at St. Just, when Mr. E. came once more, took me by the hand, and said, I must go with him. To avoid making a tumult, I went. He said, I had promised, last week, not to come again to St. Just for a month. I absolutely denied the having made any such promise. After about half an hour, he handed me back to my inn.

Riot Act and a Sermon

Wed. 10.—In the evening I began to expound (at Trevonan, in Morva), "Ho! every one that thirsteth, come ye to the waters." In less than a quarter of an hour, the constable and his companions came, and read the proclamation against riots. When he had done, I told him, "We will do as you require: we will disperse within an hour"; and went on with my sermon. After preaching, I had designed to meet the society alone. But many others also followed with such earnestness, that I could not turn them back: so I exhorted them all, to love their enemies, as Christ hath loved us. They felt what was spoken.

Thur. 25.—I came back safe, blessed be God, to Bristol. I found both my soul and body much refreshed in this peaceful place. Thursday, August 1, and the following days, we had our second Conference, with as many of our brethren that labour in the word as could be present.

Pelted by the Mob at Leeds

Mon. Sept. 9.—I left London, and the next morning called on Dr. Doddridge, at Northampton. It was about the hour when he was accustomed to expound a portion of Scripture to young gentlemen under his care. He desired me to take his place. It may be the seed was not altogether sown in vain.

Thur. 12.—I came to Leeds, preached at five, and at eight met the society; after which the mob pelted us with dirt and stones great part of the way home. The congregation was much larger next evening; and so was the mob at our return, and likewise in higher spirits, being ready to knock out all our brains for joy that the Duke of Tuscany was Emperor. What a melancholy consideration is this! that the bulk of the English nation will not suffer God to give them the blessings he would; because they would turn them into curses. He cannot, for instance, give them success against their enemies; for they would tear their own countrymen in pieces: he cannot trust them with victory, lest they should thank him by murdering those that are quiet in the land.

Great Excitement at Newcastle

Wed. 18.—About five we came to Newcastle, in an acceptable time. We found the generality of the inhabitants in the utmost consternation; news being just arrived, that, the morning before, at two o'clock, the Pretender had entered Edinburgh. A great concourse of people were with us in the evening, to whom I expounded the third chapter of Jonah; insisting particularly on that verse, " Who can tell, if God will return, and repent, and turn away from his fierce anger, that we perish not ?"

Thur. 19.—The mayor (Mr. Ridley) summoned all the householders of the town to meet him at the townhall; and desired as many of them as were willing, to set their hands to a paper, importing that they would, at the hazard of their goods and lives, defend the town against the common enemy. Fear and darkness were now on every side; but not on those who had seen the light of God's countenance. We rejoiced together in the evening with solemn joy, while God applied those words to many hearts, "Fear not ye; for I know that ye seek Jesus which was crucified."

Fri. 20.—The mayor ordered the townsmen to be under arms, and to mount guard in their turns, over and above the guard of soldiers, a few companies of whom had been drawn into the town on the first alarm. Now, also, Pilgrim-street gate was ordered to be walled up. Many began to be much concerned for us, because our house stood without the walls. Nay, but the Lord is a wall of fire unto all that trust in him.

I had desired all our brethren to join with us this day in seeking God by fasting and prayer. About one we met, and poured out our souls before him; and we believed he would send an answer of peace.

Wesley's Letter to the Mayor

Sat. 21.—The same day the action was, came the news of General Cope's defeat. Orders were now given for the doubling of the guard, and for walling up Pandon and Sally-port gates. In the afternoon I wrote the following letter:

"*To the Worshipful the Mayor of Newcastle.*

"Sir,—My not waiting upon you at the town-hall was not owing to any want of respect. I reverence you for your office' sake; and much more for your zeal in the execution of it. I would to God every magistrate in the land would copy after such an example! Much less was it owing to any disaffection to his Majesty King

George. But I knew not how far it might be either
necessary or proper for me to appear on such an occasion.
I have no fortune at Newcastle : I have only the bread
I eat, and the use of a little room for a few weeks in
the year.

"All I can do for his Majesty, whom I honour and
love—I think not less than I did my own father—is
this, I cry unto God, day by day, in public and in
private, to put all his enemies to confusion : and I
exhort all that hear me to do the same ; and, in their
several stations, to exert themselves as loyal subjects ;
who, so long as they fear God, cannot but honour the
King.

"Permit me, Sir, to add a few words more, out of the
fulness of my heart. I am persuaded you fear God,
and have a deep sense that His Kingdom ruleth over
all. Unto whom, then (I may ask you), should we flee
for succour, but unto Him whom, by our sins, we have
justly displeased ? O, Sir, is it not possible to give any
check to these overflowings of ungodliness ? to the
open, flagrant wickedness, the drunkenness and profaneness, which so abound, even in our streets ? I just take
leave to suggest this. May the God whom you serve
direct you in this, and all things ! This is the daily
prayer of, Sir,

"Your obedient servant, for Christ's sake,

"J. W."

Preaching under Difficulties.

Sun. 22.—The walls were mounted with cannon, and
all things prepared for sustaining an assault. Meantime
our poor neighbours, on either hand, were busy in
removing their goods. And most of the best houses in
our street were left without either furniture or inhabitants.

Those within the walls were almost equally busy in carrying away their money and goods; and more and more of the gentry every hour rode southward as fast as they could. At eight I preached at Gateshead, in a broad part of the street, near the Popish chapel, on the wisdom of God in governing the world. How do all things tend to the furtherance of the Gospel!

All this week the alarms from the north continued, and the storm seemed nearer every day. Many wondered we would still stay without the walls: others told us we must remove quickly; for if the cannon began to play from the top of the gates, they would beat all the house about our ears. This made me look how the cannons on the gates were planted; and I could not but adore the providence of God, for it was obvious, 1. They were all planted in such a manner, that no shot could touch our house. 2. The cannon on New-gate so secured us on one side, and those upon Pilgrim-street gate on the other, that none could come near our house, either way, without being torn in pieces.

On Friday and Saturday many messengers of lies terrified the poor people of the town, as if the rebels were just coming to swallow them up. Upon this the guards were increased, and abundance of country gentlemen came in, with their servants, horses, and arms. Among those who came from the north was one whom the mayor ordered to be apprehended, on suspicion of his being a spy. As soon as he was left alone he cut his own throat; but a surgeon coming quickly, sewed up the wound, so that he lived to discover those designs of the rebels, which were thereby effectually prevented.

Sun. 29.—Advice came that they were in full march southward, so that it was supposed they would reach Newcastle by Monday evening. At eight I called on a

multitude of sinners in Gateshead, to seek the Lord
while he might be found. Mr. Ellison preached another
earnest sermon, and all the people seemed to bend before
the Lord. In the afternoon I expounded part of the
lesson for the day—Jacob wrestling with the angel.
The congregation was so moved, that I began again and
again, and knew not how to conclude. And we cried
mightily to God to send his Majesty King George help
from his holy place, and to spare a sinful land yet a
little longer, if haply they might know the day of their
visitation.

The Blasphemous Troops

Tues. Oct. 8.—I wrote to General Husk as follows:

"A surly man came to me this evening, as he said,
from you. He would not deign to come up stairs to
me, nor so much as into the house; but stood in the
yard till I came, and then obliged me to go with him
into the street, where he said, ' You must pull down the
battlements of your house, or to-morrow the General
will pull them down for you.'

"Sir, to me this is nothing. But I humbly conceive
it would not be proper for this man, whoever he is, to
behave in such a manner to any other of his Majesty's
subjects, at so critical a time as this.

"I am ready, if it may be for his Majesty's service,
to pull not only the battlements, but the house down;
or to give up any part of it, or the whole, into your
Excellency's hands."

Sat. 26.—I sent Alderman Ridley the following letter:

" SIR,—The fear of God, the love of my country, and the
regard I have for his Majesty King George, constrain

me to write a few plain words to one who is no stranger
to these principles of action.

"My soul has been pained day by day, even in
walking the streets of Newcastle, at the senseless,
shameless wickedness, the ignorant profaneness, of the
poor men to whom our lives are entrusted. The
continual cursing and swearing, the wanton blasphemy
of the soldiers in general, must needs be a torture to the
sober ear, whether of a Christian or an honest infidel.
Can any that either fear God, or love their neighbour,
hear this without concern? especially if they consider
the interest of our country, as well as of these unhappy
men themselves. For can it be expected, that God
should be on their side who are daily affronting him to
his face? And if God be not on their side, how little
will either their number, or courage, or strength avail?

"Is there no man that careth for these souls?
Doubtless there are some who ought so to do. But
many of these, if I am rightly informed, receive large
pay, and do just nothing.

"I would to God it were in my power, in any degree,
to supply their lack of service. I am ready to do what
in me lies, to call these poor sinners to repentance, once
or twice a day (while I remain in these parts), at any
hour, or at any place. And I desire no pay at all for
doing this; unless what my Lord shall give at his
appearing.

.   .   .   .

"Having myself no knowledge of the General, I took
the liberty to make this offer to you. I have no interest
herein; but I should rejoice to serve, as I am able, my
King and country. If it be judged, that this will be of
no real service, let the proposal die, and be forgotten.
But I beg you, Sir, to believe, that I have the same

glorious cause, for which you have shown so becoming a
zeal, earnestly at heart; and that therefore I am, with
warm respect,

> " Sir,
>
> " Your most obedient servant."

Sun. 27.—I received a message from Mr. Ridley, that
he would communicate my proposal to the General, and
return me his answer as soon as possible.

Having now delivered my own soul, on Monday,
Nov. 4, I left Newcastle.   Before nine we met several
expresses, sent to countermand the march of the army
into Scotland; and to inform them, that the rebels had
passed the Tweed, and were marching southward.

Bonfires Everywhere

Tues. 5.—In the evening I came to Leeds, and found
the town full of bonfires, and people shouting, firing of
guns, cursing and swearing, as the English manner of
keeping holidays is.   I immediately sent word to some
of the magistrates, of what I had heard on the road.
This ran through the town, as it were, in an instant:
and I hope it was a token for good.   The hurry in the
streets was quashed at once—some of the bonfires
indeed remained; but scarce any one was to be seen
about them, but a few children warming their hands.

Thur. 7.—I rode to Stayley Hall, in Cheshire, after
many interruptions in the way, by those poor tools of
watchmen, who stood with great solemnity at the end of
almost every village.   I preached there on Mark i. 15,
and rode on to Bradbury Green.

Fri. 8.—Understanding that a neighbouring gentleman,
Dr. C., had affirmed to many, that Mr. Wesley was now
with the Pretender, near Edinburgh, I wrote him a few

lines. It may be, he will have a little more regard to truth, or shame, for the time to come.

Wesley and Faith-healing

1746. Mon. March 17.—I took my leave of Newcastle, and set out with Mr. Downes and Mr. Shepherd. But when we came to Smeton, Mr. Downes was so ill, that he could go no further. When Mr. Shepherd and I left Smeton, my horse was so exceeding lame that I was afraid I must have lain by too. We could not discern what it was that was amiss; and yet he would scarce set his foot to the ground. By riding thus seven miles, I was thoroughly tired, and my head ached more than it had done for some months. (What I here aver is the naked fact: let every man account for it as he sees good.) I then thought, " Cannot God heal either man or beast, by any means, or without any ? " Immediately my weariness and head-ache ceased, and my horse's lameness in the same instant. Nor did he halt any more either that day or the next. A very odd accident this also !

Fri. May 30 (Bristol).—I light upon a poor, pretty, fluttering thing, lately come from Ireland, and going to be a singer at the play-house. She went in the evening to the chapel, and thence to the watch-night, and was almost persuaded to be a Christian. Her convictions continued strong for a few days; but then her old acquaintance found her, and we saw her no more.

Sun. July 6 (London).—After talking largely with both the men and women leaders, we agreed it would prevent great expense, as well of health as of time and of money, if the poorer people of our society could be persuaded to leave off drinking of tea. We resolved ourselves to begin and set the example. I expected some difficulty in breaking off a custom of six-and-twenty years' standing. And, accordingly, the three first days, my head ached, more or less, all day long, and I was half asleep from morning till night. The third day, on Wednesday, in the afternoon, my memory failed, almost entirely. In the evening I sought my remedy in prayer. On Thursday morning my head-ache was gone. My memory was as strong as ever. And I have found no inconvenience, but a sensible benefit in several respects, from that very day to this.

Thur. 17.—I finished the little collection which I had made among my friends for a lending-stock. It did not amount to thirty pounds; which a few persons afterwards made up fifty. And by this inconsiderable sum, above two hundred and fifty persons were relieved in one year.

Wesley Encounters Severe Weather

1747. Tues. Feb. 10 (London).—My brother returned from the north, and I prepared to supply his place there. Sunday, 15. I was very weak and faint; but on Monday, 16, I rose soon after three, lively and strong, and found all my complaints were fled away like a dream.

I was wondering, the day before, at the mildness of the weather; such as seldom attends me in my journeys. But my wonder now ceased: the wind was turned full north, and blew so exceeding hard and keen, that when we came to Hatfield, neither my companions nor I had much use of our hands or feet. After resting an hour, we bore up again through the wind and snow, which drove full in our faces. But this was only a squall. In Baldock-field the storm began in earnest. The large hail drove so vehemently in our faces, that we could not see, nor hardly breathe. However, before two o'clock we reached Baldock, where one met and conducted us safe to Potten.

About six I preached to a serious congregation. Tuesday, 17. We set out as soon as it was well light; but it was really hard work to get forward; for the frost would not well bear or break; and the untracked snow covering all the roads, we had much ado to keep our horses on their feet. Meantime the wind rose higher and higher, till it was ready to overturn both man and beast. However, after a short bait at Bugden, we pushed on, and were met in the middle of an open field with so violent a storm of rain and hail, as we had not had before. It drove through our coats, great and small, boots, and everything, and yet froze as it fell, even upon our eye-brows; so that we had scarce either strength or motion left, when we came into our inn at Stilton.

We now gave up our hopes of reaching Grantham, the snow falling faster and faster. However, we took the advantage of a fair blast to set out, and made the best of our way to Stamford-heath. But here a new difficulty arose, from the snow lying in large drifts. Sometimes horse and man were well nigh swallowed np. Yet in less than an hour we were brought safe to Stamford. Being willing to get as far as we could, we made but a short stop here; and about sunset came, cold and weary, yet well, to a little town called Brig-casterton.

Wed. 18.—Our servant came up and said, "Sir, there is no travelling to-day. Such a quantity of snow has fallen in the night, that the roads are quite filled up." I told him, "At least we can walk twenty miles a day, with our horses in our hands." So in the name of God we set out. The north-east wind was piercing as a sword, and had driven the snow into such uneven heaps, that the main road was unpassable. However, we kept on, a-foot or on horseback, till we came to the White Lion at Grantham.

Some from Grimsby had appointed to meet us here; but not hearing anything of them (for they were at another house, by mistake), after an hour's rest, we set out straight for Epworth. On the road we overtook a clergyman and his servant; but the tooth-ache quite shut my mouth. We reached Newark about five.

Preaching to the Lead Miners

Tues. March 24.—I rode to Blanchland, about twenty miles from Newcastle. The rough mountains round about were still white with snow. In the midst of them is a small winding valley, through which the Derwent runs. On the edge of this the little town stands, which is indeed little more than a heap of ruins. There seems to have been a large cathedral church, by the vast walls which still remain. I stood in the churchyard, under one side of the building, upon a large tomb-stone, round which, while I was at prayers all the congregation kneeled down on the grass. They were gathered out of the lead-mines from all parts; many from Allandale, six miles off. A row of little children sat under the opposite wall, all quiet and still. The whole congregation drank in every word with such earnestness in their looks, I could not but hope that God will make this wilderness sing for joy.

Wed. June 24.—We rode (from Bristol) to Beercrocomb, hoping to reach Tavistock the next day. So we set out at three. The rain began at four. We reached Colestock, dropping wet, before seven. The rain ceased while we were in the house, but began when we took horse, and attended us all the way to Exeter. While we stayed here to dry our clothes, I took the opportunity of writing " A Word to a Freeholder." Soon after three we set out : but it was near eight before we could reach Oakhampton.

Fri. 26.—We came to Tavistock before noon ; but it being market-day, I did not preach till five in the evening. The rain began almost as soon as we began singing, and drove many out of the field. After preaching (leaving Mr. Swindells there) I went on for Plymouth-dock.

How Wesley Dealt with a Mob

Within two miles of Plymouth, one overtook and informed us, that, the night before, all the Dock was in an uproar ; and a constable, endeavouring to keep the peace, was beaten and much hurt. As we were entering the Dock, one met us, and desired we would go the back-way : " For," said he, "there are thousands of people waiting about Mr. Hide's door." We rode up straight into the midst of them. They saluted us with three huzzas ; after which I alighted, took several of them by the hand, and began to talk with them. I would gladly have passed an hour among them ; and believe, if I had, there had been an end of the riot. But the day being far spent (for it was past nine o'clock), I was persuaded to go in. The mob then recovered their spirits, and fought valiantly with the doors and windows : but about ten they were weary, and went every man to his own home.

Sat. 27.—I preached at four, and then spoke severally to part of the society. As yet I have found only one person among them who knew the love of God, before my brother came. No wonder the devil was so still ; for his goods were in peace.

About six in the evening, I went to the place where I preached the last year. A little before we had ended the hymn, came the Lieutenant, a famous man, with his retinue of soldiers, drummers, and mob. When the drums ceased, a gentleman barber began to speak: but his voice was quickly drowned in the shouts of the multitude, who grew fiercer and fiercer, as their numbers increased. After waiting about a quarter of an hour, perceiving the violence of the rabble still increasing, I walked down into the thickest of them, and took the captain of the mob by the hand. He immediately said, " Sir, I will see you safe home. Sir, no man shall touch you. Gentlemen, stand off: give back. I will knock the first man down that touches him." We walked on in great peace ; my conductor every now and then stretching out his neck (he was a very tall man) and looking round, to see if any behaved rudely, till we came to Mr. Hide's door. We then parted in much love. I stayed in the street near half an hour after he was gone, talking with the people, who had now forgot their anger, and went away in high good humour.

Sun. 28.—I preached at five, on the Common, to a well-behaved, earnest congregation : and at eight near the room, on, " Seek ye the Lord, while He may be found." The congregation was much larger than before, and equally serious and attentive. At ten I went to church. Mr. Barlow preached an useful sermon, on, " God be merciful to me a sinner " ; and a thundering one in the afternoon, on, " Where their worm dieth not, and the fire is not quenched."

Mon. 29.—I took horse between three and four, and reached Perranwell, three miles beyond Truro, about six. I preached to a very large congregation at seven ; and the word was as the rain on the tender herb.

Tues. 30.—We came to St. Ives before Morning Prayers, and walked to church without so much as one huzza. How strangely has one year changed the scene in Cornwall! This is now a peaceable, nay, honourable station. They give us good words almost in every place. What have we done, that the world should be so civil to us ?

Wed. July 1.—I spoke severally to all those who had votes in the ensuing election. I found them such as I desired. Not one would even eat or drink at the expense of him for whom he voted. Five guineas had been given to W. C., but he returned them immediately. T. M. positively refused to accept any thing. And when he heard that his mother had received money privately, he could not rest till she gave him the three guineas, which he instantly sent back.

Thursday 2, was the day of election for Parliament-men. It was begun and ended without any hurry at all. I had a large congregation in the evening, among whom two or three roared for the disquietness of their heart : as did many at the meeting which followed ; particularly those who had lost their first love.

Thurs. Aug. 13 (Dublin).—We walked in the after-noon to see two persons that were sick near Phœnix Park. That part of it which joins to the city is sprinkled up and down with trees, not unlike Hyde Park. But about a mile from the town is a thick grove of old, tall oaks ; and in the centre of this, a round, open green (from which are vistas of all four ways), with a handsome stone pillar in the midst, having a Phœnix on the top.

I continued reaching, morning and evening, to

many more than the house would contain, and had more and more reason to hope they would not all be unfruitful hearers.

Sun. Sept. 27 (London).—I preached in Moorfields, morning and evening, and continued so to do till November. I know no church in London (that in West-street excepted) where there is so serious a congregation.

Mon. 28.—I talked with one who, a little time before, was so overwhelmed with affliction, that she went out one night to put an end to it all, by throwing herself into the New River. As she went by the Foundery (it being a watch-night), she heard some people singing. She stopped, and went in ; she listened awhile, and God spoke to her heart. She had no more desire to put an end to her life; but to die to sin, and live to God.

The Bargemen and their Clubs

Mon. Nov. 2.—I preached at Windsor at noon, and in the afternoon rode to Reading. Mr. J. R. had just sent his brother word, that he had hired a mob to pull down his preaching-house that night. In the evening Mr. S. Richards overtook a large company of bargemen walking towards it, whom he immediately accosted, and asked, if they would go with him and hear a good sermon; telling them, "I will make room for you, if you were as many more." They said, they would go with all their hearts. "But neighbours," said he, "would it not be as well to leave those clubs behind you ? Perhaps some of the women may be frighted at them." They threw them all away, and walked quietly with him to the house, where he set them in a pew.

In the conclusion of my sermon, one of them who used to be their captain, being the head taller than his fellows, rose up, and looking round the congregation, said, "The gentleman says nothing but what is good; I say so; and there is not a man here that shall dare to say otherwise."

Remarkable Accident to Wesley

1748. Thur. Jan. 28.—I set out for Deverel Longbridge. About ten o'clock we were met by a loaded waggon, in a deep, hollow way. There was a narrow path between the road and the bank: I stepped into this, and John Trembath followed me. When the waggon came near, my horse began to rear, and to attempt climbing up the bank. This frighted the horse which was close behind, and made him prance and throw his head to and fro, till the bit of the bridle catched hold of the cape of my great coat, and pulled me backward off my horse. I fell as exact on the path, between the waggon and the bank, as if one had taken me in his arms and laid me down there. Both our horses stood stock still, one just behind me, the other before; so, by the blessing of God, I rose unhurt, mounted again, and rode on.

Sat. Feb. 6.—I preached at eight in the morning at Bath, and in the evening at Coleford. The colliers of this place were "darkness" indeed; but now they are "light in the Lord."

Tues. 9.—I met about sixty of the society in Bristol, to consult about enlarging the room; and indeed securing it, for there was no small danger of its falling upon our heads. In two or three days, two hundred and thirty pounds were subscribed. We immediately procured experienced builders to make an estimate of the expense; and I appointed five stewards (besides those of the society) to superintend the work,

Fri. 12.—After preaching at Oakhill about noon, I rode to Shepton, and found them all under a strange consternation. A mob, they said, was hired, prepared, and made sufficiently drunk, in order to do all manner of mischief. I began preaching between four and five : none hindered or interrupted at all. We had a blessed opportunity, and the hearts of many were exceedingly comforted. I wondered what was become of the mob. But we were quickly informed : they mistook the place, imagining I should alight (as I used to do) at William Stone's house, and had summoned, by drum, all their forces together, to meet me at my coming : but Mr. Mr. Swindells innocently carrying me to the other end of the town, they did not find their mistake till I had done preaching : so that the hindering this, which was one of their designs, was utterly disappointed.

However, they attended us from the preaching-house to William Stone's, throwing dirt, stones, and clods, in abundance : but they could not hurt us ; only Mr. Swindells had a little dirt on his coat, and I a few specks on my hat.

A Shower of Stones

After we were gone into the house, they began throwing great stones, in order to break the door. But perceiving this would require some time, they dropped that design for the present. They first broke all the tiles on the pent-house over the door, and then poured in a shower of stones at the windows. One of their captains, in his great zeal, had followed us into the house, and was now shut in with us. He did not like this, and would fain have got out ; but it was not possible ; so he kept as close to me as he could, thinking himself safe when he was near me : but, staying a little behind—when I went up two pair of stairs, and stood close on one side, where we were a little sheltered —a large stone struck him on the forehead, and the blood spouted out like a stream. He cried out, " O Sir, are we to die to-night? What must I do? What must I do?" I said, " Pray to God. He is able to deliver you from all danger." He took my advice, and began praying in such a manner as he had scarce done ever since he was born.

Mr. Swindells and I then went to prayer; after which I told him, " We must not stay here; we must go down immediately." He said, " Sir, we cannot stir; you see how the stones fly about." I walked straight through the room, and down the stairs; and not a stone came in, till we were at the bottom. The mob had just broke open the door when we came into the lower room; and exactly while they burst in at one door, we walked out at the other. Nor did one man take any notice of us, though we were within five yards of each other.

A Horrible Proposition

They filled the house at once, and proposed setting it on fire. But one of them, happening to remember that his own house was next, with much ado persuaded them not to do it. Hearing one of them cry out, " They are gone over the grounds," I thought the advice was good; so we went over the grounds, to the farther end of the town, where Abraham Jenkins waited, and undertook to guide us to Oakhill.

I was riding on in Shepton Lane, it being now quite dark, when he cried out, " Come down: come down from the bank." I did as I was bid; but the bank being high, and the side very near perpendicular, I came down all at once, my horse and I tumbling one over another. But we both rose unhurt.

Sat. April 9.—I preached in Connaught, a few miles from Athlone.   Many heard; but, I doubt, felt nothing.

The Shannon comes within a mile of the house where I preached.   I think there is not such another river in Europe: it is here ten or twelve miles over, though scarce thirty miles from its fountain-head.   There are many islands in it, once well inhabited, but now mostly desolate.   In almost every one is the ruins of a church: in one, the remains of no less than seven.   I fear, God hath still a controversy with this land, because it is defiled with blood.

Incidents in Ireland

Sun. 10 (Easter-day).—Never was such a congregation seen before at the sacrament in Athlone.   I preached at three.   Abundance of Papists flocked to hear; so that the priest, seeing his command did not avail, came in person at six, and drove them away before him like a flock of sheep.

Tues. 12.—I rode to Clara, where I was quickly informed, that there was to begin in an hour's time a famous cockfight, to which almost all the country was coming from every side.   Hoping to engage some part of them in a better employ, I began preaching in the street, as soon as possible.   One or two hundred stopped, and listened a while, and pulled off their hats, and forgot their diversion.

The congregation at Tullamore in the evening was larger than ever before, and deep attention sat on every face.   Toward the latter end of the sermon, there began a violent storm of hail.   I desired the people to cover their heads; but the greater part of them would not; nor did any one go away till I concluded my discourse.

Fri. 15.—I rode to Edinderry.   Abundance of people

were quickly gathered together.   Having been disturbed
in the night by Mr. Swindells, who lay with me, and had
a kind of apoplectic fit, I was not at all well about noon,
when I began to preach, in a large walk, on one side of
the town, and the sun shone hot upon my head, which
had been aching all the day; but I forgot this before I
had spoken long ; and when I had finished my discourse,
I left all my weariness and pain behind, and rode on, in
perfect health to Dublin.

Sat. 23.—I read, some hours, an extremely dull book,
Sir James Ware's " Antiquities of Ireland."   By the vast
number of ruins which are seen in all parts, I had
always suspected what he shows at large, namely, that in
ancient times it was more populous, tenfold, than it is
now; many that were large cities, being now ruinous
heaps; many shrunk into inconsiderable villages.

I visited one in the afternoon who was ill of a fever,
and lay in a very close room.   While I was near him, I
found myself not well.   After my return home, I felt
my stomach out of order.   But I imagined it was not
worth any notice, and would pass off before the morning.

Wesley Lives on Apple-tea

Sun. 24.—I preached at Skinner's Alley at five ; and
on Oxmantown Green at eight.   I was weak in body,
but was greatly revived by the seriousness and earnestness
of the congregation.   Resolving to improve the opportunity, I gave notice of preaching there again in the
afternoon ; which I did to a congregation much more
numerous, and equally attentive.   As I came home I
was glad to lie down, having a quinsey, attended with a
fever.   However, when the society met, I made a shift
to creep in among them.   Immediately my voice was
restored.   I spoke without pain, for near an hour

together. And great was our rejoicing over each other ; knowing that God would order all things well.

Mon. 25.—Finding my fever greatly increased, I judged it would be best to keep my bed, and to live awhile on apples and apple-tea. On Tuesday I was quite well, and should have preached, but that Dr. Rutty (who had been with me twice) insisted on my resting for a time.

I read to-day what is accounted the most correct history of St. Patrick that is extant ; and, on the maturest consideration, I was much inclined to believe, that St. Patrick and St. George were of one family. The whole story smells strong of romance.

A Determined Preacher

Thursday, 28, was the day fixed for my going into the country : but all about me began to cry out, " Sure, you will not go to-day ? See how the rain pours down ! " I told them, " I must keep my word, if possible." But before five, the man of whom I had bespoke an horse sent word, his horse should not go out in such a day. I sent one who brought him to a better mind. So about six I took horse. About nine I called at Killcock.

Between one and two we came to Kinnegad. My strength was now pretty well exhausted ; so that when we mounted again, after resting an hour, it was as much as I could do to sit my horse. We had near eleven Irish (measured) miles to ride, which are equal to fourteen English. I got over them pretty well in three hours, and by six reached Tyrrel's Pass.

At seven I recovered my strength, so as to preach and meet the society ; which began now to be at a stand, with regard to number, but not with regard to the grace of God.

Fri. 29.—I rode to Temple Maqueteer, and thence toward Athlone. We came at least an hour before we were expected. Nevertheless we were met by many of our brethren. The first I saw, about two miles from the town, were a dozen little boys running with all their might, some bare-headed, some bare-footed and bare-legged : so they had their desire of speaking to me first, the others being still behind.

Zealous Protestants

Tues. May 3.—I rode to Birr, twenty miles from Athlone, and, the key of the sessions-house not being to be found, declared " the grace of our Lord Jesus Christ " in the street, to a dull, rude, senseless multitude. Many laughed the greater part of the time. Some went away just in the middle of a sentence. And yet when one cried out (a Carmelite friar, clerk to the priest), "You lie ! you lie ! " the zealous Protestants cried out, "Knock him down " : and it was no sooner said than done. I saw some bustle, but knew not what was the matter, till the whole was over.

In the evening we rode to Balliboy. There being no house that could contain the congregation, I preached here also in the street. I was afraid, in a new place, there would be but few in the morning ; but there was a considerable number, and such a blessing as I had scarce found since I landed in Ireland.

Sun. 15 (Dublin).—Finding my strength greatly restored, I preached at five, and at eight on Oxman-town Green. I expected to sail as soon as I had done ; but the captain putting it off (as their manner is), gave me an opportunity of declaring the Gospel of peace to a still larger congregation in the evening. One of them, after listening some time, cried out, shaking his head,

" Ay, he is a Jesuit ; that's plain." To which a Popish priest, who happened to be near, replied aloud, " No, he is not ; I would to God he was."

Mon. 16.—Observing a large congregation in the evening, and many strangers among them, I preached more roughly than ever I had done in Dublin, on those awful words, " What shall it profit a man, if he shall gain the whole world, and lose his own soul ? "

Wed. 18.—We took ship. The wind was small in the afternoon, but exceeding high towards night. About eight I laid me down on the quarter-deck. I was soon wet from head to foot, but I took no cold at all. About four in the morning we landed at Holyhead, and in the evening reached Carnarvon.

Fri. August 12.—In riding to Newcastle, I finished the tenth Iliad of Homer. What an amazing genius had this man ! To write with such strength of thought, and beauty of expression, when he had none to go before him ! And what a vein of piety runs through his whole work, in spite of his pagan prejudices ! Yet one cannot but observe such improprieties intermixed, as are shocking to the last degree.

Wesley Protests Against Lawlessness

Thur. 25.—I rode with Mr. Grimshaw to Roughlee. At half-hour after twelve I began to preach. I had about half finished my discourse, when the mob came pouring down the hill like a torrent. After exchanging a few words with their captain, to prevent any contest, I went with him as he required. When we came to Barrowford, two miles off, the whole army drew up in battle array before the house into which I was carried, with two or three of my friends. After I had been detained above an hour, their captain went out, and I followed him, and desired him to conduct me whence I came. He said, he would : but the mob soon followed after ; at which he was so enraged, that he must needs turn back to fight them, and so left me alone.

A farther account is contained in the following letter, which I wrote the next morning—

Widdop, Aug. 26, 1748.

" Sir,—Yesterday, between twelve and one o'clock, while I was speaking to some quiet people, without any noise or tumult, a drunken rabble came, with clubs and staves, in a tumultuous and riotous manner, the captain of whom, Richard B., by name, said he was a deputy-constable, and that he was come to bring me to you. I went with him ; but I had scarce gone ten yards, when a man of his company struck me with his fist in the face with all his might ; quickly after, another threw his stick at my head : I then made a little stand ; but another of your champions, cursing and swearing in the most shocking manner, and flourishing his club over his head, cried out, ' Bring him away ! '

" With such a convoy I walked to Barrowford, where they informed me you was ; their drummer going before, to draw all the rabble together from all quarters.

" When your deputy had brought me into the house, he permitted Mr. Grimshaw, the minister of Haworth, Mr. Colbeck, of Keighley, and one more, to be with me, promising that none should hurt them. Soon after you and your friends came in, and required me to promise, I would come to Roughlee no more. I told you, I would sooner cut off my hand, than make any such promise : neither would I promise that none of my friends should come. After abundance of rambling discourse (for I could keep none of you long to any one

point), from about one o'clock till between three and
four (in which one of you frankly said, 'No ; we will
not be like Gamaliel, we will proceed like the Jews '), you
seemed a little satisfied with my saying, ' I will not
preach at Roughlee at this time.' You then undertook
to quiet the mob, to whom you went and spoke a few
words, and their noise immediately ceased. I then
walked out with you at the back-door.

Beaten by the Mob

" I should have mentioned that I had several times
before desired you to let me go, but in vain ; and that
when I attempted to go with Richard B., the mob
immediately followed, with oaths, curses, and stones ;
that one of them beat me down to the ground ; and
when I rose again, the whole body came about me like
lions, and forced me back into the house.

" While you and I went out at one door, Mr. Grimshaw and Mr. Colbeck went out at the other. The mob
immediately closed them in, tossed them to and fro with
the utmost violence, threw Mr. Grimshaw down, and
loaded them both with dirt and mire of every kind ;
not one of your friends offering to call off your blood-
hounds from the pursuit.

" The other quiet, harmless people, who followed me
at a distance, to see what the end would be, they treated
still worse ; not only by the connivance, but by the
express order, of your deputy. They made them run
for their lives, amidst showers of dirt and stones, without any regard to age or sex. Some of them they
trampled in the mire, and dragged by the hair, particularly
Mr. Mackford, who came with me from Newcastle.
Many they beat with their clubs without mercy. One
they forced to leap down (or they would have thrown

him headlong) from a rock, ten or twelve feet high, into the river.   And when he crawled out, wet and bruised, they swore they would throw him in again, which they were hardly persuaded not to do.   All this time you sat well-pleased close to the place, not attempting in the least to hinder them.

"And all this time you was talking of justice and law !   Alas, Sir, suppose we were Dissenters (which I deny), suppose we were Jews or Turks, are we not to have the benefit of the laws of our country ?   Proceed against us by the law, if you can or dare; but not by lawless violence ; not by making a drunken, cursing, swearing, riotous mob, both judge, jury, and executioner. This is flat rebellion against God and the King, as you may possibly find to your cost."

Defending Field Preaching

Between four and five we set out from Roughlee. But observing several parties of men upon the hills, and suspecting their design, we put on and passed the lane they were making for before they came.   One of our brothers, not riding so fast, was intercepted by them. They immediately knocked him down, and how it was that he got from amongst them he knew not.

Before seven we reached Widdop.   The news of what had passed at Barrowford made us all friends.   The person in whose house Mr. B. preached, sent and begged I would preach there ; which I did at eight, to such a congregation as none could have expected on so short a warning.   He invited us also to lodge at his house, and all jealousies vanished away.

Sun. 28.—I was invited by Mr. U., the Minister ot Goodshaw, to preach in his church.   I began reading prayers at seven; but perceiving the church would scarce contain half of the congregation, after prayers I went out, and standing on the churchyard wall, in a place shaded from the sun, explained and enforced those words in the second lesson, " Almost thou persuadest me to be a Christian."

I wonder at those who still talk so loud of the indecency of field-preaching. The highest indecency is in St. Paul's Church, when a considerable part of the congregation are asleep, or talking, or looking about, not minding a word the preacher says. On the other hand, there is the highest decency in a churchyard or field, when the whole congregation behave and look as if they saw the Judge of all, and heard Him speaking from heaven.

Three Remarkable Shots with Stones

At one I went to the Cross in Bolton. There was a vast number of people, but many of them utterly wild. As soon as I began speaking, they began thrusting to and fro; endeavouring to throw me down from the steps on which I stood. They did so once or twice; but I went up again, and continued my discourse. They then began to throw stones; at the same time some got upon the Cross behind me to push me down; on which I could not but observe, how God overrules even the minutest circumstances. One man was bawling just at my ear, when a stone struck him on the cheek, and he was still. A second was forcing his way down to me, till another stone hit him on the forehead : it bounded back, the blood ran down, and he came no farther. The third, being got close to me, stretched out his hand, and in the instant a sharp stone came upon the joints of his fingers. He shook his hand, and was very quiet till I concluded my discourse and went away.

Sat. Oct. 22.—I spent an hour in observing the various works of God in the Physic Garden at Chelsea. It would be a noble improvement of the design, if some able and industrious person were to make a full and accurate inquiry into the use and virtues of all these plants : without this, what end does the heaping them thus together answer, but the gratifying an idle curiosity ?

Mon. Nov. 21.—I set out for Leigh, in Essex. It had rained hard in the former part of the night, which was succeeded by a sharp frost; so that most of the road was like glass; and the north-east wind set just in our face. However, we reached Leigh by four in the afternoon. Here was once a deep open harbour; but the sands have long since blocked it up, and reduced a once flourishing town to a small ruinous village. I preached to most of the inhabitants of the place in the evening; to many in the morning, and then rode back to London.

Wesley in Wales

1749. Mon. April 3.—I set out for Ireland. We waited more than four hours at the passage; by which delay, I was forced to disappoint a large congregation at Newport. About three I came to Pedras, near Carphilly. The congregation had waited some hours. I began immediately, wet and weary as I was; and we rejoiced over all our labours.

In the evening, and the next morning (Tues. 4), I preached at Cardiff. O what a fair prospect was here some years ago ! Surely this whole town would have known God, from the least even to the greatest, had it not been for men leaning to their own understanding, instead of " the law and the testimony."

At twelve I preached at Lanmais, to a loving, earnest

people, who do not desire to be any wiser than God. In the evening I preached at Fonmon, the next morning at Cowbridge. How is the scene changed since I was here last, amidst the madness of the people, and the stones flying on every side! Now all is calm; the whole town is in good humour, and flock to hear the glad tidings of salvation. In the evening I preached at Lantrissent.

Thursday, 6. We rode to a hard-named place on the top of a mountain. I scarce saw any house near: however, a large number of honest, simple people soon came together; but few could understand me: so Henry Lloyd, when I had done, repeated the substance of my sermon in Welsh. The behaviour of the people recompensed us for our labour in climbing up to them.

Marries his Brother

About noon we came to Aberdare, just as the bell was ringing for a burial. This had brought a great number together, to whom, after the burial, I preached in the church. We had almost continued rain from Aberdare to the great rough mountain that hangs over the vale of Brecknock: but as soon as we gained the top of this, we left the clouds behind us. We had a mild, fair, sunshiny evening the remainder of our journey.

Fri. 7.—We reached Garth. Saturday, 8. I married my brother and Sarah Gwynne. It was a solemn day, such as becomes the dignity of a Christian marriage.

Wed. 12.—We came to Holyhead between one and two. But all the ships were on the Irish side. One came in the next day, but could not go out, the wind being quite contrary. In this journey I read over Statius's Thebais. I wonder one man should write so

well and so ill. Sometimes he is scarce inferior to
Virgil; sometimes as low as the dullest parts of Ovid.

In the evening I preached on, " Be ye also ready."
The poor people now seemed to be much affected; and
equally so the next night: so that I was not sorry that
the wind was contrary.

Sat. 15.—We went on board at six, the wind then
standing due east. But no sooner were we out of the
harbour, than it turned south-west, and blew a storm.
Yet we made forward, and about one o'clock came
within two or three leagues of land. The wind then
wholly failed; a calm suddenly following a storm,
produced such a motion as I never felt before. But it
was not long before the wind sprung up west, which
obliged us to stand away for the Skerries. When we
wanted a league of shore it fell calm again, so that there
we rolled about till past sunset.

But in the night we got back into Dublin Bay, and
landed soon after three at Dunleary, about seven English
miles from the city. Leaving William Tucker to follow me
in a chaise, I walked straight away, and came to Skinner's
Alley a little before the time of preaching. I preached
on, " Beloved, if God so loved us, we ought also to love
one another." In the afternoon, and again in the
evening (in our own garden), I preached on, " Let us
come boldly unto the throne of grace, that we may
obtain mercy, and find grace to help in time of need."

On Thursday and Friday I examined the classes, and
was much comforted among them. I left about four
hundred in the society; and, after all the stumbling-
blocks laid in the way, I found four hundred and forty-
nine.

Mon. 24.—The cold which I had had for some days
growing worse and worse, and the swelling which began

in my cheek increasing greatly, and paining me much, I sent for Dr. Rutty. But, in the mean time, I applied boiled nettles, which took away the pain in a moment. Afterwards I used warm treacle, which so abated the swelling, that before the doctor came I was almost well. However, he advised me not to go out that day. But I had appointed to read the letters in the evening. I returned home as early as I could, and found no inconvenience.

Methodists Lease an Abbey

Fri. May 12.—Before nine we came to Nenagh. I had no design to preach; but one of the dragoons quartered there, would take no denial : so I ordered a chair to be carried out, and went to the market-place. Presently such a congregation was gathered round me as I had not seen since I left Athlone. To these I spake, as I was able, the whole counsel of God; and then rode cheerfully on to Limerick.

Between six and seven I preached at Mardyke (an open place without the walls), to about two thousand people; not one of whom I observed either to laugh, or to look about, or to mind anything but the sermon.

Some years since an old abbey here was rebuilt, with a design to have public service therein. But that design failing, only the shell of it was finished. Of this (lying useless) the society has taken a lease. Here I preached in the morning, Saturday, 13, to six or seven hundred people.

We then went to prayers at the cathedral, an ancient and venerable pile. In the afternoon I walked round the walls of the town, scarce so large as Newcastle-upon-Tyne. And the fortifications are much in the same repair ; very sufficient to keep out the wild Irish.

14.—(Being Whit-Sunday). Our church was more than full in the morning, many being obliged to stand without. I hardly knew how the time went, but continued speaking till near seven o'clock. I went at eleven to the cathedral. I had been informed it was a custom here, for the gentry especially, to laugh and talk all the time of divine service; but I saw nothing of it. The whole congregation, rich and poor, behaved suitably to the occasion.

In the evening I preached to a numerous congregation, on, "If any man thirst, let him come unto me and drink." We afterwards met the society. Six or seven prisoners of hope were set at liberty this day.

Mon. 15.—A company of revellers and dancers had in the afternoon taken possession of the place where I used to preach. Some advised me to go to another place; but I knew it needed not. As soon as ever I came in sight, the holiday mob vanished away.

Wesley and the Soldiers' Class

Wed. 17.—I met the class of soldiers, eight of whom were Scotch Highlanders. Most of these were brought up well; but evil communications had corrupted good manners. They all said, from the time they entered into the army, they had grown worse and worse. But God had now given them another call, and they knew the day of their visitation.

Mon. 22.—The more I converse with this people, the more I am amazed. That God hath wrought a great work among them, is manifest; and yet the main of them, believers and unbelievers, are not able to give a rational account of the plainest principles of religion. It is plain, God begins His work at the heart; then "the inspiration of the Highest giveth understanding."

Wed. 24.—About eight, several of us took boat for Newtown, six miles from Limerick. After dinner we took boat, in order to return. The wind was extremely high. We endeavoured to cross over to the leeward side of the river; but it was not possible. The boat being small, and over-loaded, was soon deep in water; the more so, because it leaked much, and the waves washed over us frequently; and there was no staying to empty it, all our men being obliged to row with all their strength. After they had toiled about an hour, the boat struck upon a rock, the point of which lay just under the water. It had four or five shocks, the wind driving us on before we could get clear. But our men wrought for life; and about six o'clock God brought us safe to Limerick.

A Ridiculous Question

Mon. June 5.—I rode to Blarney, three miles wide of Cork, where many of the society met me. I spent some time with them in exhortation and prayer, and then went on to Rathcormuck.

I was a little surprised at the acuteness of a gentleman here, who in conversation with Colonel Barry, about late occurrences, said, he had heard, there was a people risen up that placed all religion in wearing long whiskers; and seriously asked, whether these were not the same who were called Methodists.

Tues. 13.—We rode over to Gloster, a beautiful seat built by an Englishman, who had scarce finished his house, and laid out his gardens, when he was called to his everlasting home. Sir L—— P—— and his lady dined with us, whether coming by accident or design I know not. About five I preached in the stately saloon, to a little company of plain, serious people; the fine

ones looking on, and some of them seeming to be a
little affected. I expounded at Birr about seven, in
the strongest manner I could, the story of Dives and
Lazarus.

Wed. 14.—We designed to dine at Ferbane, about
twelve miles from Birr. We stopped at the first inn
in the town; but they did not care to entertain heretics;
neither did the people at the second inn; I alighted
at the third, and went in, without asking any questions.

About seven I preached at Athlone. It being the
time of the general review, abundance of soldiers and
many officers were present. They all behaved with
the utmost decency. But a gentleman of the town
did not; which had like to cost him dear. Many
swords were drawn; but the officers interposed, and it
went no farther.

Wed. July 19.—I finished the translation of " Martin
Luther's Life." Doubtless he was a man highly favoured
of God, and a blessed instrument in His hand. But O!
what pity that he had no faithful friend! None that
would, at all hazards, rebuke him plainly and sharply,
for his rough, untractable spirit, and bitter zeal for
opinions, so greatly obstructive of the work of God!

A Rough Voyage

Thur. 20.—About ten at night we embarked [from
Dublin] for Bristol, in a small sloop. I soon fell asleep.
When I awaked in the morning, we were many leagues
from land, in a rough, pitching sea. Toward evening
the wind turned more against us, so that we made little
way. About ten we were got between the Bishop and
his Clerks (the rocks so called) and the Welsh shore;
the wind blew fresh from the south; so that the
captain, fearing we should be driven on the rocky coast,

steered back again to sea. On Saturday morning we made the Bishop and his Clerks again, and beat to and fro all the day. About eight in the evening it blew hard, and we had a rolling sea: notwithstanding which, at four on Sunday morning, we were within sight of Minehead. The greatest part of the day we had a dead calm; but in the evening the wind sprung up, and carried us into Kingroad. On Monday morning we landed at the quay in Bristol.

Tues. 25.—I rode over to Kingswood, and inquired particularly into the state of our school there. I was concerned to find that several of the rules had been habitually neglected: I judged it necessary, therefore, to lessen the family; suffering none to remain therein, who were not clearly satisfied with them, and determined to observe them all.

Wed. Sept. 6.—I reached Newcastle; and after resting a day, and preaching two evenings and two mornings, with such a blessing as we have not often found, on Friday set out to visit the northern societies. I began with that at Morpeth, where I preached at twelve, on one side of the market-place. It was feared the market would draw the people from the sermon; but it was just the contrary: they quitted their stalls, and there was no buying or selling till the sermon was concluded.

At Alnwick likewise I stood in the market-place in the evening, and exhorted a numerous congregation to be always ready for death, for judgment, for heaven. I felt what I spoke; as I believe did most that were present, both then and in the morning, while I besought them to " present " themselves, "a living sacrifice, holy, acceptable to God."

Sat. 9.—I rode slowly forward to Berwick. I was myself much out of order; but I would not lose the opportunity of calling, in the evening, all that were "weary and heavy-laden," to Him who hath said, "I will give you rest."

Tues. 26.—I had a solemn and delightful ride to Keswick, having my mind stayed on God.

Wed. 27.—I took horse at half an hour past three. There was no moon, or stars, but a thick mist; so that I could see neither road, nor anything else; but I went as right as if it had been noon-day. When I drew nigh Penruddock Moor, the mist vanished, the stars appeared, and the morning dawned; so I imagined all the danger was past; but when I was on the middle of the moor, the mist fell again on every side, and I quickly lost my way. I lifted up my heart. Immediately it cleared up, and I soon recovered the high-road. On Alstone Moor I missed my way again; and what, I believe, no stranger has done lately, rode through all the bogs, without any stop, till I came to the vale, and thence to Hinely Hill.

A large congregation met in the evening. I expounded part of the twentieth chapter of the Revelation. But O what a time was this! It was as though we were already standing before the "great white throne." God was no less present with us in prayer; when one just by me cried with a loud and bitter cry. I besought God to give us a token that all things should work together for good. He did so: he wrote pardon upon her heart; and we all rejoiced unto him with reverence.

Wed. Oct. 18.—I rode, at the desire of John Bennet, to Rochdale, in Lancashire. As soon as ever we entered the town, we found the streets lined on both sides with multitudes of people, shouting, cursing, blaspheming, and gnashing upon us with their teeth. Perceiving it would not be practicable to preach abroad, I

went into a large room, open to the street, and called
aloud, " Let the wicked forsake his way, and the un-
righteous man his thoughts." The word of God
prevailed over the fierceness of man. None opposed or
interrupted ; and there was a very remarkable change
in the behaviour of the people, as we afterwards went
through the town.

Remarkable Scenes at Bolton

We came to Bolton about five in the evening. We
had no sooner entered the main street, than we perceived the lions at Rochdale were lambs in comparison
of those at Bolton. Such rage and bitterness I scarce
ever saw before, in any creatures that bore the form of
men. They followed us in full cry to the house where
we went ; and as soon as we were gone in, took possession of all the avenues to it, and filled the street from
one end to the other.

After some time the waves did not roar quite so loud.
Mr. P—— thought he might then venture out. They
immediately closed in, threw him down, and rolled him
in the mire ; so that when he scrambled from them, and
got into the house again, one could scarce tell what or
who he was. When the first stone came among us
through the window, I expected a shower to follow ; and
the rather, because they had now procured a bell to call
their whole forces together. But they did not design to
carry on the attack at a distance : presently one ran up
and told us, the mob had burst into the house : he
added, that they had got J—— B—— in the midst of
them. They had ; and he laid hold on the opportunity
to tell them of " the terrors of the Lord."

Meantime D—— T—— engaged another part of
them with smoother and softer words. Believing the

time was now come, I walked down into the thickest of them. They had now filled all the rooms below. I called for a chair. The winds were hushed, and all was calm and still. My heart was filled with love, my eyes with tears, and my mouth with arguments. They were amazed, they were ashamed, they were melted down, they devoured every word. What a turn was this! O how did God change the counsel of the old Ahithophel into foolishness; and bring all the drunkards, swearers, Sabbath-breakers, and mere sinners in the place, to hear of His plenteous redemption!

Thur. 19.—Abundantly more than the house could contain were present at five in the morning, to whom I was constrained to speak a good deal longer than I am accustomed to do. Perceiving they still wanted to hear, I promised to preach again at nine, in a meadow near the town. Thither they flocked from every side; and I called aloud, "All things are ready; come unto the marriage." O how have a few hours changed the scene! We could now walk through every street of the town, and none molested or opened his mouth, unless to thank or bless us.

Wesley at Dudley and Birmingham

On Tuesday, 24, about noon, we came to Dudley. At one I went to the market-place, and proclaimed the name of the Lord to an huge, unwieldy, noisy multitude; the greater part of whom seemed in no wise to know "wherefore they were come together." I continued speaking about half an hour, and many grew serious and attentive, till some of Satan's servants pressed in, raging and blaspheming, and throwing whatever came to hand. I then retired to the house from which I came. The multitude poured after, and

covered over with dirt many that were near me ; but I
had only a few specks.   I preached in Wednesbury at
four, to a nobler people, and was greatly comforted
among them : so I was likewise in the morning, Wednesday, 25.   How does a praying congregation strengthen
the preacher !

After preaching again at one, I rode to Birmingham.
This had been long a dry uncomfortable place ; so I
expected little good here : but I was happily disappointed.
Such a congregation I never saw there before : not a
scoffer, nor a trifler, not an inattentive person (so far as
I could discern) among them ; and seldom have I known
so deep, solemn a sense of the power, and presence, and
love of God.   The same blessing we had at the meeting
of the society ; and again at the morning preaching.
Will then God at length cause even this barren wilderness to blossom and bud as the rose ?

Wesley in Wales

1750. Sun. Jan. 28.—I read prayers (in London),
and Mr. Whitefield preached.   How wise is God in
giving different talents to different preachers !   Even
the little improprieties both of his language and manner
were a means of profiting many, who would not have
been touched by a more correct discourse, or a more
calm and regular manner of speaking.

Tues. March 6 (Bristol).—I began writing a short
French Grammar.   We observed Wednesday, 7, as a
day of fasting and prayer.

Sun. 11.—I should willingly have spent more time
in Bristol ; finding more and more proofs that God was
reviving His work ; but that the accounts I received
from Ireland made me think it my duty to be there as
soon as possible ; so, on Monday, 19, I set out with

M

Christopher Hopper for the New Passage. When we came there, the wind was high, and almost full against us : nevertheless we crossed in less than two hours, and reached Cardiff before night ; where I preached at seven, and found much refreshment.

Tues. 20.—Expecting to preach at Aberdare, sixteen Welsh miles from Cardiff, I rode thither over the mountains. But we found no notice had been given : so, after resting an hour, we set out for Brecknock. The rain did not intermit at all, till we came within sight of it. Twice my horse fell down, and threw me over his head ; but without any hurt, either to man or beast.

Wed. 21.—We rode to Builth, where we found notice had been given, that Howell Harris would preach at noon. By this means a large congregation was assembled ; but Howell did not come : so, at their request, I preached. Between four and five Mr. Philips set out with us for Royader. I was much out of order in the morning : however, I held out to Llanidloes, and then lay down. After an hour's sleep I was much better, and rode on to Machynlleth.

About an hour and a half before we came to Dolgelly, the heavy rain began. We were on the brow of the hill, so we took all that came, our horses being able to go but half a foot-pace. But we had amends made us at our inn : John Lewis, and all his house, gladly joined with us in prayer ; and all we spoke to appeared willing to hear and to receive the truth in love.

Fri. 23.—Before we looked out, we heard the roaring of the wind, and the beating of the rain. We took horse at five. It rained incessantly all the way we rode. And when we came on the great mountain, four miles from the town (by which time I was wet from my neck

to my waist), it was with great difficulty I could avoid
being borne over my mare's head, the wind being ready
to carry us all away: nevertheless, about ten we came
safe to Dannabull, praising Him who saves both man
and beast.

Our horses being well tired, and ourselves thoroughly
wet, we rested the remainder of the day; the rather,
because several of the family understood English—an
uncommon thing in these parts. We spoke closely to
these; and they appeared much affected, particularly
when we all joined in prayer.

Waiting for the Irish Boat

Sat. 24.—We set out at five, and at six came to the
sands. But the tide was in, so that we could not pass:
so I sat down in a little cottage for three or four hours,
and translated Aldrich's " Logic." About ten we passed,
and before five came to Baldon Ferry, and found the
boat ready for us: but the boatmen desired us to stay
a while, saying, the wind was too high, and the tide too
strong. The secret was, they stayed for more passengers;
and it was well they did: for while we were walking to
and fro, Mr. Jenkin Morgan came; at whose house,
near half-way between the ferry and Holyhead, I had
lodged three years before. The night soon came on;
but our guide, knowing all the country, brought us safe
to his own door.

Sun. 25.—I preached at Howell Thomas's, in
Trefollwin parish, to a small, earnest congregation.

The wind being contrary, I accepted of the invitation
of an honest exciseman (Mr. Holloway), to stay at his
house till it should change. Here I was in a little,
quiet, solitary spot, where no human voice was heard,
but those of the family. On Tuesday I desired Mr.

Hopper to ride over to Holyhead, and inquire concerning our passage. He brought word, that we might probably pass in a day or two: so on Wednesday we both went thither. Here we overtook John Jane, who had set out on foot from Bristol with three shillings in his pocket. Six nights out of the seven since he set out, he had been entertained by utter strangers. He went by us we could not tell how, and reached Holyhead on Sunday, with one penny left.

By him we sent back our horses to Mr. Morgan's. I had a large congregation in the evening. It almost grieved me, I could give them but one sermon, now they were at length willing to hear. About eleven we were called to go on board, the wind being quite fair: and so it continued till we were just out of the harbour. It then turned west, and blew a storm. There was neither moon nor stars, but rain and wind enough; so that I was soon tired of staying on deck. But we met another storm below: for who should be there, but the famous Mr. Gr——, of Carnarvonshire—a clumsy, overgrown, hard-faced man; whose countenance I could only compare to that (which I saw in Drury Lane thirty years ago) of one of the ruffians in "Macbeth." I was going to lie down, when he tumbled in, and poured out such a volley of ribaldry, obscenity, and blasphemy, every second or third word being an oath, as was scarce ever heard at Billingsgate. Finding there was no room for me to speak, I retired into my cabin, and left him to Mr. Hopper. Soon after, one or two of his own company interposed, and carried him back to his cabin.

Thur. 29.—We wrought our way four or five leagues toward Ireland; but were driven back in the afternoon to the very mouth of the harbour; nevertheless the wind shifting one or two points, we ventured out again; and by midnight we were got about half seas over; but the wind then turning full against us, and blowing hard, we were driven back again, and were glad, about nine, to get into the bay once more.

In the evening I was surprised to see, instead of some poor, plain people, a room full of men, daubed with gold and silver. That I might not go out of their depth, I began expounding the story of Dives and Lazarus. It was more applicable than I was aware; several of them (as I afterwards learned) being eminently wicked men. I delivered my own soul; but they could in nowise bear it. One and another walked away, murmuring sorely. Four stayed till I drew to a close; they then put on their hats, and began talking to one another. I mildly reproved them; on which they rose up and went away, railing and blaspheming. I had then a comfortable hour with a company of plain, honest Welshmen.

"Where is the Parson?"

In the night there was a vehement storm. Blessed be God that we were safe on shore! Saturday, 31. I determined to wait one week longer, and, if we could not sail then, to go and wait for a ship at Bristol. At seven in the evening, just as I was going down to preach, I heard a huge noise, and took knowledge of the rabble of gentlemen. They had now strengthened themselves with drink and numbers, and placed Captain Gr—— (as they called him) at their head. He soon burst open both the outward and inner door, struck old Robert Griffith, our landlord, several times, kicked his wife, and, with twenty full-mouthed oaths and curses, demanded, "Where is the parson?" Robert Griffith came up, and desired me to go into another room, where he locked me in. The captain followed him quickly, broke open one or two doors, and got on a chair, to look on the top of a bed : but his foot slipping (as he was not a man made for climbing), he fell down backward all his length. He rose leisurely, turned about, and, with his troop, walked away.

I then went down to a small company of the poor people, and spent half an hour with them in prayer. About nine, as we were preparing to go to bed, the house was beset again. The captain burst in first. Robert Griffith's daughter was standing in the passage with a pail of water, with which (whether with design or in her fright, I know not) she covered him from head to foot. He cried as well as he could, "M—urder! Murder!" and stood very still for some moments. In the mean time Robert Griffith stepped by him and locked the door. Finding himself alone, he began to change his voice, and cry, "Let me out! Let me out!" Upon his giving his word and honour, that none of the rest should come in, they opened the door, and all went away together.

Wesley Interviews Mrs. Pilkington

Thur. April 12 (Dublin).—I breakfasted with one of the society, and found she had a lodger I little thought of. It was the famous Mrs. Pilkington, who soon made an excuse for following me up stairs. I talked with her seriously about an hour : we then sung, "Happy Magdalene." She appeared to be exceedingly struck : how long the impression may last, God knows.

Sun. May 20 (Cork).—Understanding the usual place of preaching would by no means contain those who desired to hear, about eight I went to Hammond's

Marsh. The congregation was large and deeply attentive. A few of the rabble gathered at a distance; but
by little and little they drew near, and mixed with the
congregation: so that I have seldom seen a more
quiet and orderly assembly at any church in England or
Ireland.

In the afternoon, a report being spread abroad that
the mayor designed to hinder my preaching on the
Marsh in the evening, I desired Mr. Skelton and Mr.
Jones to wait upon him, and inquire concerning it.
Mr. Skelton asked, if my preaching there would be
disagreeable to him; adding, "Sir, if it would, Mr.
Wesley will not do it." He replied warmly, "Sir, I'll
have no mobbing." Mr. Skeleton replied, "Sir, there
was none this morning." He answered, "There was.
Are there not churches and meeting-houses enough?
I will have no more mobs or riots." Mr. Skelton
replied, "Sir, neither Mr. Wesley nor they that heard
him made either mobs or riots." He answered plain,
"I will have no more preaching; and if Mr. Wesley
attempts to preach, I am prepared for him."

I began preaching in our own house soon after five.
Mr. Mayor meantime was walking in the 'Change, and
giving orders to the town-drummers and to his sergeants
—doubtless to go down and keep the peace! They
accordingly came down to the house, with an innumerable mob attending them. They continued drumming,
and I continued preaching, till I had finished my discourse. When I came out, the mob immediately closed
me in. Observing one of the sergeants standing by, I
desired him to keep the King's peace; but he replied,
"Sir, I have no orders to do that." As soon as I came
into the street, the rabble threw whatever came to hand;
but all went by me, or flew over my head; nor do I

remember that one thing touched me. I walked on straight through the midst of the rabble, looking every man before me in the face; and they opened on the right and left, till I came near Dant's Bridge. A large party had taken possession of this, one of whom was bawling out, "Now, hey for the Romans!" When I came up, they likewise shrunk back, and I walked through them to Mr. Jenkins's house; but a Papist stood just within the door, and endeavoued to hinder my going in; till one of the mob (I suppose aiming at me, but missing) knocked her down flat. I then went in, and God restrained the wild beasts, so that not one attempted to follow me.

But many of the congregation were more roughly handled, particularly Mr. Jones, who was covered with dirt, and escaped with his life almost by miracle. The main body of the mob then went to the house, brought out all the seats and benches, tore up the floor, the door, the frames of the windows, and whatever of wood-work remained; part of which they carried off for their own use, and the rest they burnt in the open street.

Finding there was no probability of their dispersing, I sent to Alderman Pembrock, who immediately desired Mr. Alderman Windthrop, his nephew, to go down to Mr. Jenkins, with whom I walked up the street, none giving me an unkind or disrespectful word.

Wesley Burnt in Effigy

Mon. 21.—I rode on to Bandon. From three in the afternoon till past seven, the mob of Cork marched in grand procession, and then burnt me in effigy near Dant's Bridge.

Wed. 23.—The mob was still patrolling the streets, abusing all that were called Methodists, and threatening to murder them and pull down their houses, if they did not leave this way.

Thur. 24.—They again assaulted Mr. Stockdale's house, broke down the boards he had nailed up against the windows, destroyed what little remained of the window-frames and shutters, and damaged a considerable part of his goods.

Fri. 25.—One Roger O'Ferrall fixed up an advertisement at the public Exchange, that he was ready to head any mob, in order to pull down any house that should dare to harbour a swaddler. (A name given to Mr. Cennick first by a Popish priest, who heard him speak of a child wrapped in swaddling clothes; and probably did not know the expression was in the Bible, a book he was not much acquainted with.)

At this time God gave us great peace at Bandon, notwithstanding the unwearied labours, both public and private, of good Dr. B.———, to stir up the people. But, Saturday, 26, many were under great apprehensions of what was to be done in the evening. I began preaching in the main street at the usual hour, but to more than twice the usual congregation. After I had spoke about a quarter of an hour, a clergyman, who had planted himself near me, with a very large stick in his hand, according to agreement, opened the scene. (Indeed his friends assured me he was in drink, or he would not have done it.) But, before he had uttered many words, two or three resolute women, by main strength, pulled him into a house; and, after expostulating a little, sent him away through the garden.

The next champion that appeared was one Mr. M———, a young gentleman of the town. He was attended by two others, with pistols in their hands. But his triumph too was but short; some of the people quickly bore him away, though with much gentleness and civility.

The third came on with greater fury; but he was encountered by a butcher of the town (not one of the Methodists), who used him as he would an ox, bestowing one or two hearty blows upon his head. This cooled his courage, especially as none took his part. So I quietly finished my discourse.

Visits to Kinsale and Cork

Mon. 28.—I rode to Kinsale, one of the pleasantest towns which I have seen in Ireland. At seven I preached at the Exchange, to a few gentry, many poor people, and abundance of soldiers. All behaved like men that feared God. After sermon came one from Cork, and informed us Mr. W—— had preached both morning and afternoon under the wall of the barracks; that the town-drummers came; but the soldiers assured them if they went to beat there they would be all cut in pieces; that then the mayor came himself, at the head of his mob, but could make no considerable disturbance; that he went and talked to the commanding officer, but with so little success, that the colonel came out and declared to the mob, they must make no riot there. Here is a turn of affairs worthy of God! Doth He not rule in heaven and earth?

Wed. 30.—I rode to Cork. By talking with Captain ——, I found there was no depending on the good offices of the colonel. He had told the captain with great openness, "If Mr. Wesley preached in the barracks, and the mob were to come and break the windows, I might have a long bill from the barrack-master." Break the windows! Nay, it is well if they had not broken the bones of all the soldiers.

A little before five I walked towards the barracks. The boys quickly gathered, and were more and more turbulent. But in a moment all was quiet. This, I afterwards found, was owing to Mr. W———, who snatched a stick out of a man's hand, and brandished it over his head, on which the whole troop valiantly ran away.

When we came over the south bridge, a large mob gathered; but before they were well formed we reached the barrack gate; at a small distance from which I stood and cried, "Let the wicked forsake his way." The congregation of serious people was large; the mob stood about a hundred yards off. I was a little surprised to observe, that almost all the soldiers kept together in a body near the gate, and knew not but the report might be true, that, on a signal given, they were all to retire into the barracks; but they never stirred until I had done. As we walked away, one or two of them followed us. Their numbers increased, until we had seven or eight before and a whole troop of them behind; between whom I walked, through an immense mob, to Alderman Pembrock's door.

At an Irish Funeral

Thurs. 31.—I rode to Rathcormuck. There being a great burying in the afternoon, to which people came from all parts, Mr. Lloyd read part of the burial service in the church; after which I preached on, " The end of all things is at hand." I was exceedingly shocked at (what I had only heard of before) the Irish howl which followed. It was not a song, as I supposed, but a dismal, inarticulate yell, set up at the grave by four shrill-voiced women, who (we understood) were hired for that purpose. But I saw not one that shed a tear; for that it seems, was not in their bargain.

Wed. June 13.—I rode to Shronill again ; and in the morning, Thursday, 14, to Clonmell. After an hour's rest we set forward, but were obliged to stop in the afternoon, sooner than we designed, by my horse having a shoe loose. The poor man, at whose house we called, was not only patient of exhortation, but exceeding thankful for it. We afterwards missed our way ; so that it was near eight o'clock before we got over the ferry, a mile short of Waterford.

At the ferry was a lad who asked my name. When he heard it, he cried out, "O Sir, you have no business here ; you have nothing to do at Waterford. Butler has been gathering mobs there all this week ; and they set upon us so, that we cannot walk the streets. But if you will stay at that little house, I will go and bring B. M'Cullock to you."

We stayed some time, and then thought it best to go a little on our way toward Portarlington. But the ferryman would not come over : so that, after waiting till we were weary, we made our way through some grounds, and over the mountain, into the Carrick road ; and went on, about five miles, to a village where we found a quiet house. Sufficient for this day was the labour thereof. We were on horseback, with but an hour or two's intermission, from five in the morning, till within a quarter of eleven at night.

Fri. 15.—About two in the morning I heard people making a great noise, and calling me by my name. They were some of our friends from Waterford, who informed us, that, upon the lad's coming in, sixteen or eighteen of them came out, to conduct me into the town. Not finding me, they returned ; but the mob met them by the way, and pelted them with dirt and stones to their own doors.

We set out at four, and reached Kilkenny, about twenty-five old Irish miles, about noon. This is by far the most pleasant, as well as most fruitful country, which I have seen in all Ireland. Our way after dinner lay by Dunmore, the seat of the late Duke of Ormond. We rode through the park for about two miles, by the side of which the river runs. I never saw either in England, Holland, or Germany, so delightful a place. The walks, each consisting of four rows of ashes, the tufts of trees sprinkled up and down, interspersed with the smoothest and greenest lawns, are beautiful beyond description. And what hath the owner thereof, the Earl of Arran? Not even the beholding it with his eyes.

Wesley Rides Ninety Miles

My horse tired in the afternoon; so I left him behind, and borrowed that of my companion. I came to Aymo about eleven, and would very willingly have passed the rest of the night there; but the good woman of the inn was not minded that I should. For some time she would not answer: at last she opened the door just wide enough to let out four dogs upon me. So I rode on to Ballybrittas, expecting a rough salute here too, from a large dog which used to be in the yard. But he never stirred, till the hostler waked and came out. About twelve I laid me down. I think this was the longest day's journey I ever rode; being fifty old Irish, that is, about ninety English miles.

Thurs. 21.—I returned to Closeland, and preached in the evening to a little, earnest company. O who should drag me into a great city, if I did not know there is another world! How gladly could I spend the remainder of a busy life in solitude and retirement!

Thur. Sept. 6.—I rode to Salisbury and preached at Winterburn in the evening; the next, at Reading; and, on Saturday, 8, came to London.

Here I had the following account from one of our preachers :—

"John Jane was never well after walking from Epworth to Hainton, on an exceeding hot day, which threw him into a fever. But he was in great peace and love, even to those who greatly wanted love to him. He was some time at Alice Shadforth's house, with whom he daily talked of the things of God. He was never without the love of God, spent much time in private prayer, and joined likewise with her in prayer several times in a day. On Friday, August 24, growing, as she thought, stronger in body, he sat in the evening by the fire-side : about six he fetched a deep sigh, and never spoke more. He was alive till the same hour on Saturday; at which, without any struggle, or any sign of pain, with a smile on his face, he passed away. His last words were, ' I find the love of God in Christ Jesus.'

He Left One Shilling and Fourpence

"All his clothes, linen and woollen, stockings, hat, and wig, are not thought sufficient to answer his funeral expenses, which amount to one pound seventeen shillings and threepence. All the money he had was one shilling and fourpence." Enough for any unmarried preacher of the Gospel to leave to his executors.

Mon. 17.—My brother set out for the north; but returned the next day, much out of order. How little do we know the counsels of God! But we know they are all wise and gracious.

Wed. 19.—When I came home in the evening, I found my brother abundantly worse. He had had no

sleep for several nights ; and expected none, unless from
opiates. I went down to our brethren below, and we
made our request known to God. When I went up
again he was in a sound sleep, which continued till the
morning.

Fri. 21.—We had a watch-night at Spitalfields. I
often wonder at the peculiar providence of God on these
occasions. I do not know that in so many years one
person has ever been hurt, either in London, Bristol, or
Dublin, in going so late in the night to and from all
parts of the town.

Sun. 23.—My brother being not yet able to assist, I
had more employment to-day than I expected. In the
morning I read prayers, preached, and administered the
sacrament to a large congregation in Spitalfields. The
service at West Street continued from nine till one. At
five I called the sinners in Moorfields to repentance.
And, when I had finished my work found more liveliness
and strength than I did at six in the morning.

Wesley as Editor

Mon. 24.—I left London, and, the next morning,
called at what is styled the Half-way House. Quickly
after, as a young man was riding by the door, both horse
and man tumbled over each other. As soon as he got
up, he began cursing his horse. I spoke a few words,
and he was calm. He told me, he did fear God once ;
but for some time past he had cared for nothing. He
went away full of good resolutions. God bring them to
good effect !

I reached Kingswood in the evening ; and the next
day selected passages of Milton for the eldest children
to transcribe and repeat weekly.

Thur. 27.—I went into the school, and heard half the

children their lessons, and then selected passages of the "Moral and Sacred Poems." Friday, 28. I heard the other half of the children. Saturday, 29. I was with them from four to five in the morning. I spent most of the day in revising Kennet's "Antiquities," and marking what was worth reading in the school.

Wed. Oct. 3.—I revised, for the use of the children, Archbishop Potter's "Grecian Antiquities"; a dry, dull, heavy book. Thursday, 4. I revised Mr. Lewis's "Hebrew Antiquities"; something more entertaining than the other, and abundantly more instructive.

Sat. 6.—I nearly finished the abridgment of Dr. Cave's "Primitive Christianity"; a book wrote with as much learning, and as little judgment, as any I remember to have read in my whole life; serving the ancient Christians just as Xenophon did Socrates; relating every weak thing they ever said or did.

Thur. 11.—I prepared a short "History of England," for the use of the children; and on Friday and Saturday a short "Roman History," as an introduction to the Latin historians.

Mon. 15.—I read over Mr. Holmes's "Latin Grammar"; and extracted from it what was needful to perfect our own.

In Canterbury Cathedral

Mon. Dec. 3.—I rode to Canterbury, and preached on Rev. xx. A few turbulent people made a little noise, as I found it was their custom to do. Perceiving more of them were gathered the next night, I turned and spoke to them at large. They appeared to be not a little confounded, and went away as quiet as lambs.

Wed. 5.—I walked over the cathedral, and surveyed the monuments of the ancient men of renown. One

would think such a sight should strike an utter damp
upon human vanity. What are the great, the fair, the
valiant now? the matchless warrior—the puissant
monarch?—

> An heap of dust is all remains of thee!
> 'Tis all thou art, and all the proud shall be.

Mon. 10.—I rode to Leigh, in Essex, where I found
a little company seeking God; and endeavoured to
encourage them in "provoking one another to love and
good works."

Mon. 17.—I set upon cleansing Augeas's stable;
upon purging that huge work, Mr. Fox's "Acts and
Monuments," from all the trash which that honest,
injudicious writer has heaped together, and mingled
with those venerable records, which are worthy to be had
in everlasting remembrance.

1751. Wed. Jan. 30.—Having received a pressing
letter from Dr. Isham, then the rector of our college,
to give my vote at the election for a Member of Parliament, which was to be the next day, I set out early, in a
severe frost, with the north-west wind full in my face.
The roads were so slippery, that it was scarce possible
for our horses to keep their feet: indeed one of them
could not; but fell upon his head, and cut it terribly.
Nevertheless, about seven in the evening, God brought
us safe to Oxford. A congregation was waiting for me
at Mr. Evans's, whom I immediately addressed in those
awful words, "What is a man profited, if he shall gain
the whole world, and lose his own soul?"

Thur. 31.—I went to the schools, where the Convo-
cation was met: but I did not find the decency and
order which I expected. The gentleman for whom I
came to vote was not elected: yet I did not repent of

N

my coming; I owe much more than this to that generous, friendly man, who now rests from his labours.

I was much surprised wherever I went, at the civility of the people—gentlemen as well as others. There was no pointing, no calling of names, as once; no, nor even laughter. What can this mean? Am I become a servant of men? Or is the scandal of the cross ceased?

Wesley Decides to Marry

Fri. Feb. 1.—We set out for London in another bitter morning, having such a wind (now got to the east, and so in our face again) as I hardly ever remember. But by five in the evening we were under shelter at the Foundery. It being the night before appointed for a watch-night, we continued praying and praising God as usual, till about twelve o'clock: and I found no inconvenience, but a little faintness, which a few hours' sleep removed.

Sat. 2.—Having received a full answer from Mr. P——, I was clearly convinced that I ought to marry. For many years I remained single because I believed I could be more useful in a single, than in a married state. And I praise God, who enabled me so to do. I now as fully believed, that in my present circumstances, I might be more useful in a married state; into which, upon this clear conviction, and by the advice of my friends, I entered a few days after.

Wed. 6.—I met the single men, and showed them on how many accounts it was good for those who had received that gift from God, to remain "single for the kingdom of heaven's sake"; unless where a particular case might be an exception to the general rule.

Sun. 10.—After preaching at five, I was hastening to take my leave of the congregation at Snowsfields, purposing to set out in the morning for the north; when, on the middle of London-bridge, both my feet slipped on the ice, and I fell with great force, the bone of my ankle lighting on the top of a stone. However, I got on, with some help, to the chapel, being resolved not to disappoint the people. After preaching, I had my leg bound up by a surgeon, and made a shift to walk to the Seven Dials. It was with much difficulty that I got up into the pulpit; but God then comforted many of our hearts.

I went back in a coach to Mr. B——'s, and from thence in a chair to the Foundery; but I was not able to preach, my sprain growing worse. I removed to Threadneedle Street; where I spent the remainder of the week, partly in prayer, reading, and conversation, partly in writing an "Hebrew Grammar," and "Lessons for Children."

Sun. 17.—I was carried to the Foundery, and preached, kneeling (as I could not stand), on part of the twenty-third Psalm; my heart being enlarged, and my mouth opened to declare the wonders of God's love.

Marriage and Preaching

Monday, 18, was the second day I had appointed for my journey; but I was disappointed again, not being yet able to set my foot to the ground. However, I preached (kneeling) on Tuesday evening, and Wednesday morning.

Sun. 24.—I preached, morning and evening, at Spitalfields.

Mon. Mar. 4.—Being tolerably able to ride, though not to walk, I set out for Bristol. I came thither on Wednesday, thoroughly tired; though, in other respects, better than when I set out.

Tues. 19.—Having finished the business for which I came to Bristol, I set out again for London; being desired by many to spend a few days there before I entered upon my northern journey. I came to London on Thursday, and, having settled all affairs, left it again on Wednesday, 27. I cannot understand, how a Methodist preacher can answer it to God, to preach one sermon, or travel one day less, in a married than in a single state. In this respect surely, " it remaineth, that they who have wives be as though they had none."

Wesley and his Barber

Thur. April 11 (Bolton).—The barber who shaved me said, " Sir, I praise God on your behalf. When you was at Bolton last, I was one of the most eminent drunkards in all the town; but I came to listen at the window, and God struck me to the heart. I then earnestly prayed for power against drinking; and God gave me more than I asked: he took away the very desire of it. Yet I felt myself worse and worse, till, on April 5 last, I could hold out no longer. I knew I must drop into hell that moment, unless God appeared to save me: and he did appear. I knew he loved me; and felt sweet peace. Yet I did not dare to say I had faith, till, yesterday was twelvemonth, God gave me faith; and his love has ever since filled my heart."

Mon. 22.—The rain stopped while I was preaching at the market-place in Morpeth. We rode from thence to Alnwick, where (it being too wet to preach at the Cross) some of our friends procured the Town Hall. This, being very large, contained the people well; only the number of them made it extremely hot.

Tues. 23.—We rode on to Berwick-upon-Tweed.

Wed. 24.—Mr. Hopper and I took horse between three and four, and about seven came to Old-camus. Whether the country was good or bad we could not see, having a thick mist all the way. The Scotch towns are like none which I ever saw, either in England, Wales, or Ireland : there is such an air of antiquity in them all, and such a peculiar oddness in their manner of building. But we were most surprised at the entertainment we met with in every place, so far different from common report. We had all things good, cheap, in great abundance, and remarkably well-dressed. In the afternoon we rode by Preston Field, and saw the place of battle, and Colonel Gardiner's house. The Scotch here affirm, that he fought on foot after he was dismounted, and refused to take quarter. Be it as it may, he is now " where the wicked cease from troubling, and where the weary are at rest."

Wesley's Impressions of Scotland

We reached Musselburgh between four and five. I had no intention to preach in Scotland; nor did I imagine there were any that desired I should. But I was mistaken. Curiosity (if nothing else) brought abundance of people together in the evening. And whereas in the kirk (Mrs. G—— informed me) there used to be laughing and talking, and all the marks of the grossest inattention : but it was far otherwise here : they remained as statues from the beginning of the sermon to the end.

Thur. 25.—We rode to Edinburgh ; one of the dirtiest cities I had ever seen, not excepting Cölen in Germany.

We returned to Musselburgh to dinner, whither we were followed in the afternoon by a little party of gentlemen from Edinburgh. I know not why any should complain of the shyness of the Scots toward strangers. All I spoke with were as free and open with me as the people of Newcastle or Bristol; nor did any person move any dispute of any kind, or ask me any question concerning my opinion.

I preached again at six, on, "Seek ye the Lord, while He may be found." I used great plainness of speech toward them; and they all received it in love: so that the prejudice which the devil had been several years planting was torn up by the roots in one hour. After preaching, one of the bailies of the town, with one of the elders of the kirk, came to me, and begged I would stay with them a while, if it were but two or three days, and they would fit up a far larger place than the school, and prepare seats for the congregation. Had not my time been fixed, I should gladly have complied.

Wesley's Remarkable Vitality

1752. Sun. March 15 (London).—While I was preaching at West Street in the afternoon, there was one of the most violent storms I ever remember. In the midst of the sermon great part of an house opposite to the chapel was blown down. We heard an huge noise, but knew not the cause; so much the more did God speak to our hearts: and great was the rejoicing of many in confidence of his protection. Between four and five I took horse, with my wife and daughter. The tiles were rattling from the houses on both sides; but they hurt not us. We reached Hayes about seven in the evening, and Oxford the next day.

Thur. April 16.—I walked over to Burnham. I had no thought of preaching there, doubting if my strength would allow of preaching always thrice a day, as I had done most days since I came from Evesham. But finding an house full of people, I could not refrain. Still the more I use my strength, the more I have. I am often much tired the first time I preach in a day ; a little the second time ; but after the third or fourth, I rarely feel either weakness or weariness.

Wed. 22.—I rode to Grimsby. The crowd was so great in the evening, that the room was like an oven. The next night I preached at the end of the town, whither almost all the people, rich and poor, followed me ; and I had a fair opportunity of closely applying that weighty question, " Lord, are there few that be saved ? "

Fri. 24.—We rode by a fine seat ; the owner of which (not much above fourscore years old) says he desires only to live thirty years longer ; ten to hunt, ten to get money (having at present but twenty thousand pounds a year), and ten years to repent. O that God may not say unto him, " Thou fool, this night shall thy soul be required of thee ! "

When I landed at the quay in Hull, it was covered with people, inquiring, " Which is he ? Which is he ? " But they only stared and laughed ; and we walked un-molested to Mr. A——'s house.

I was quite surprised at the miserable condition of the fortifications ; far more ruinous and decayed than those at Newcastle, even before the rebellion. It is well there is no enemy near.

A Crowded Coach

I went to prayers at three in the old church—a grand and venerable structure. Between five and six the coach called, and took me to Mighton Car, about half a mile from the town. An huge multitude, rich and poor, horse and foot, with several coaches, were soon gathered together ; to whom I cried with a loud voice and a composed spirit, " What shall it profit a man, if he shall gain the whole world, and lose his own soul ? " Some thousands of the people seriously attended ; but many behaved as if possessed by Moloch. Clods and stones flew about on every side ; but they neither touched nor disturbed me.

When I had finished my discourse, I went to take coach ; but the coachman had driven clear away. We were at a loss, till a gentlewoman invited my wife and me to come into her coach. She brought some inconveniences on herself thereby ; not only as there were nine of us in the coach, three on each side, and three in the middle ; but also as the mob closely attended us, throwing in at the windows (which we did not think it prudent to shut) whatever came next to hand. But a large gentlewoman who sat in my lap, screened me, so that nothing came near me.

Wesley Sleeps in a Cellar

Mon. May 25.—We rode to Durham, and thence, through very rough roads, and as rough weather, to Barnard Castle. I was exceeding faint when we came in : however, the time being come, I went into the street, and would have preached ; but the mob was so numerous and so loud, that it was not possible for many to hear. Nevertheless, I spoke on, and those who were near listened with huge attention. To prevent this, some of the rabble fetched the engine, and threw a good deal of water on the congregation ; but not a drop fell on me. After about three quarters of an hour, I returned into the house.

Tues. June 9.—My lodging was not such as I should have chosen ; but what Providence chooses is always good. My bed was considerably under ground, the room serving both for a bed-chamber and a cellar. The closeness was more troublesome at first than the cool-ness : but I let in a little fresh air, by breaking a pane of paper (put by way of glass) in the window ; and then slept sound till the morning.

Mon. 15.—I had many little trials in this journey, of a kind I had not known before. I had borrowed a young, strong mare, when I set out from Manchester. But she fell lame before I got to Grimsby. I procured another, but was dismounted again between Newcastle and Berwick. At my return to Manchester, I took my own : but she had lamed herself in the pasture. I thought, nevertheless, to ride her four or five miles to-day ; but she was gone out of the ground, and we could hear nothing of her. However, I comforted myself, that I had another at Manchester, which I had lately bought. But when I came thither, I found one had borrowed her too, and rode her away to Chester.

Sat. 20.—I rode to Chester, and preached at six, in the accustomed place, a little without the gates, near St. John's church. One single man, a poor alehouse-keeper, seemed disgusted, spoke a harmless word, and ran away with all speed. All the rest behaved with the utmost seriousness, while I declared " the grace of our Lord Jesus Christ."

Round Chester Walls

Mon. 22.—We walked round the walls of the city, which are something more than a mile and three quarters in circumference. But there are many vacant spaces within the walls, many gardens, and a good deal o pasture-ground : so that I believe Newcastle-upon-Tyne, within the walls, contains at least a third more houses than Chester.

The greatest convenience here is what they call "the Rows"; that is, covered galleries, which run through the main streets on each side, from east to west, and from north to south; by which means one may walk both clean and dry in any weather, from one end of the city to the other.

I preached, at six in the evening, in the square, to a vast multitude, rich and poor. The far greater part, the gentry in particular, were seriously and deeply attentive; though a few of the rabble, most of them drunk, laboured much to make a disturbance. One might already perceive a great increase of earnestness in the generality of the hearers.

Tues. Aug. 25.—I preached in the market-place at Kinsale. The next morning, at eight, I walked to the fort. On the hill above it we found a large, deep hollow, capable of containing two or three thousand people. On one side of this, the soldiers soon cut a place with their swords for me to stand, where I was screened both from the wind and sun, while the congregation sat on the grass before me. Many eminent sinners were present, particularly of the army; and I believe God gave them a loud call to repentance.

Sat. Sept. 23.—We reached Cork. Sunday, 24. In the evening I proposed to the society the building a preaching-house. The next day ten persons subscribed an hundred pounds; another hundred was subscribed in three or four days, and a piece of ground taken. I saw a double providence now in our not sailing last week. If we had, probably this house had never been built; and it is most likely we should have been cast away. Above thirty ships, we were informed, have been lost on these coasts in the late storm.

The wind being contrary still, on Monday, Oct. 2, I rode once more to Bandon. But though I came unexpected, the house was too small to contain one half of the congregation; so I preached in the street, both this evening, and at five on Tuesday morning; the moon giving us as much light as we wanted, till the sun supplied her place. I then returned to Cork. On Friday, 6, the ship being under sail, we took boat, and came to Cove in the evening. All the inns being full, we lodged at a private house; but we found one inconvenience herein: we had nothing to eat; for our provisions were on board, and there was nothing to be bought in the town; neither flesh, nor fish, nor butter, nor cheese. At length we procured some eggs and bread, and were well contented.

A Boiling Sea

Sun. 8.—We were called early by the pilot, and told we must rise and go on board. We did so, and found a large number of passengers: but the wind turning, most of them went on shore. At eleven I preached to those that were left. About six it blew a storm: but we were anchored in a safe harbour; so it neither hurt nor disturbed us.

Mon. 9.—Finding there was no probability of sailing soon, we went up to Mr. P——'s, near Passage. I preached there in the street about four, to most of the inhabitants of the town. They behaved very quietly; but very few seemed either convinced or affected.

Tues. 10.—We had another violent storm: it made Mr. P——'s house rock to and fro, though it was a new, strong house, and covered on all sides with hills, as well

as with trees.   We afterwards heard, that several ships
were lost on the coast.   Only one got into the harbour,
but grievously shattered, her rigging torn in pieces, and
her main-mast gone by the board.

Wed. 11.—I rode to Cork once more, and was very
fully employed all the day.   The next morning we
returned to Cove, and about noon got out of the
harbour.   We immediately found the effects of the late
storm, the sea still boiling like a pot.   The moon set
about eight, but the Northern Lights abundantly supplied her place.   Soon after, God smoothed the face of
the deep, and gave us a small, fair wind.

Fri. 13.—I read over Pascal's "Thoughts."   What
could possibly induce such a creature as Voltaire to give
such an author as this a good word; unless it was, that
he once wrote a satire?   And so his being a satirist
might atone even for his being a Christian.

Sat. 14.—About seven we sailed into Kingroad, and
happily concluded our little voyage.   I now rested a
week at Bristol and Kingswood, preaching only morning
and evening.

Wesley's Forgiveness

Sunday, 29, was an useful day to my soul.   I found
more than once trouble and heaviness; but I called
upon the name of the Lord; and he gave me a clear,
full approbation of his way, and a calm, thankful
acquiescence in his will.

I cannot but stand amazed at the goodness of God.
Others are most assaulted on the weak side of their
soul; but with me it is quite otherwise; if I have any
strength at all (and I have none but what I have
received), it is in forgiving injuries; and on this very
side am I assaulted, more frequently than on any other.

Yet leave me not here one hour to myself, or I shall betray myself and Thee!

In the remaining part of this (November), and in the following month, I prepared the rest of the books for the " Christian Library "; a work by which I have lost about two hundred pounds. Perhaps the next generation may know the value of it.

1753. Sat. Jan. 20.—I advised one who had been troubled many years with a stubborn paralytic disorder, to try a new remedy. Accordingly, she was electrified, and found immediate help. By the same means I have known two persons cured of an inveterate pain in the stomach; and another of a pain in his side, which he had had ever since he was a child. Nevertheless, who can wonder that many gentlemen of the faculty, as well as their good friends, the apothecaries, decry a medicine so shockingly cheap and easy, as much as they do quick-silver and tar-water?

Sat. Feb. 3.—I visited one in the Marshalsea prison; a nursery of all manner of wickedness. O shame to man, that there should be such a place, such a picture of hell, upon earth! And shame to those who bear the name of Christ, that there should need any prison at all in Christendom!

Thur. 8.—A proposal was made for devolving all temporal business, books and all, entirely on the Stewards; so that I might have no care upon me (in London at least) but that of the souls committed to my charge. O when shall it once be! From this day?

In the afternoon I visited many of the sick; but such scenes, who could see unmoved? There are none such to be found in a pagan country. If any of the Indians in Georgia were sick (which indeed exceeding rarely happened, till they learned gluttony and drunkenness from the Christians), those that were near him gave him whatever he wanted. O who will convert the English into honest Heathens!

On Friday and Saturday I visited as many more as I could. I found some in their cells under ground; others in their garrets, half starved both with cold and hunger, added to weakness and pain. But I found not one of them unemployed, who was able to crawl about the room. So wickedly, devilishly false is that common objection, "They are poor, only because they are idle." If you saw these things with your own eyes, could you lay out money in ornaments or superfluities?

Thur. 15.—I visited Mr. S——, slowly recovering from a severe illness. He expressed much love, and did not doubt, he said, inasmuch as I meant well, but that God would convince me of my great sin in writing books; seeing men ought to read no book but the Bible. I judged it quite needless to enter into a dispute with a sea captain, seventy-five years old.

Fri. March 16.—I returned to Bristol; and on Monday, 19, set out with my wife for the north.

Sat. 31.—I preached at Boothbank, where I met Mr. C——, late gardener to the Earl of W——. Surely it cannot be! Is it possible the earl should turn off an honest, diligent, well-tried servant, who had been in the family above fifty years, for no other fault than hearing the Methodists?

Sun. April 15.—I preached in the afternoon at Cockermouth, to well nigh all the inhabitants of the town. Intending to go from thence into Scotland, I inquired concerning the road, and was informed, I could not pass the arm of the sea which parts the two kingdoms, unless I was at Bonas, about thirty miles from Cockermouth, soon after five in the morning. At first

I thought of taking an hour or two's sleep, and setting out at eleven or twelve. But, upon farther consideration, we chose to take our journey first, and rest afterward. So we took horse about seven, and having a calm, moonshiny night, reached Bonas before one. After two or three hours' sleep, we set out again, without any faintness or drowsiness.

The Pay of Preaching

Our landlord, as he was guiding us over the Frith, very innocently asked, how much a year we got by preaching thus. This gave me an opportunity of explaining to him that kind of gain which he seemed utterly a stranger to. He appeared to be quite amazed, and spake not one word, good or bad, till he took his leave.

Presently after he went, my mare stuck fast in a quagmire, which was in the midst of the high road. But we could well excuse this ; for the road all along, for near fifty miles after, was such as I never saw any natural road, either in England or Ireland ; nay, far better, notwithstanding the continued rain, than the turnpike road between London and Canterbury.

We dined at Dumfries, a clean, well-built town, having two of the most elegant churches (one at each end of the town) that I have seen. We reached Thorny Hill in the evening. What miserable accounts pass current in England of the inns in Scotland! Yet here, as well as wherever we called in our whole journey, we had not only everything we wanted, but everything readily and in good order, and as clean as I ever desire.

Tues. 17.—We set out about four, and rode over several high, but extremely pleasant, mountains, to

Lead Hill; a village of miners, resembling Placey, near Newcastle. We dined at a village called Lesmahaggy, and about eight in the evening reached Glasgow. A gentleman who had overtaken us on the road sent one with us to Mr. Gillies's house.

Wesley in Glasgow

Wed. 18.—I walked over the city, which I take to be as large as Newcastle-upon-Tyne. The University (like that of Dublin) is only one College, consisting of two small squares; I think not larger, nor at all handsomer, than those of Lincoln College, in Oxford. The habit of the students gave me surprise. They wear scarlet gowns, reaching only to their knees. Most I saw were very dirty, some very ragged, and all of very coarse cloth. The high church is a fine building. The outside is equal to that of most cathedrals in England; but it is miserably defaced within; having no form, beauty, or symmetry left.

At seven in the evening Mr. G. began the service, at his own (the College) church. It was so full before I came, that I could not get in without a good deal of difficulty.

Thur. 19.—At seven I preached about a quarter of a mile from the town; but it was an extremely rough and blustering morning; and few people came either at the time or place of my preaching: the natural consequence of which was, that I had but a small congregation. About four in the afternoon, a tent, as they term it, was prepared; a kind of moving pulpit, covered with canvass at the top, behind, and on the sides. In this I preached near the place where I was in the morning, to near six times as many people as before; and I am persuaded what was spoken came to some of their hearts, "not in word only, but in power."

Fri. 20.—I had designed to preach at the same place ; but the rain made it impracticable. So Mr. G. desired me to preach in his church ; so I began between seven and eight. Surely with God nothing is impossible ! Who would have believed, five-and-twenty years ago, either that the minister would have desired it, or that I should have consented to preach in a Scotch kirk ?

Apprenticeship Customs

Wed. 25.—We came to Alnwick on the day whereon those who have gone through their apprenticeship are made free of the corporation. Sixteen or seventeen, we were informed, were to receive their freedom this day, and, in order thereto (such is the unparalleled wisdom of the present corporation, as well as of their forefathers), to walk through a great bog (purposely preserved for the occasion ; otherwise it might have been drained long ago), which takes up some of them to the neck, and many of them to the breast.

Tues. May 8.—I rode [from Stockton] to Robinhood's Bay, near Whitby. The town is very remarkably situated : it stands close to the sea, and is in great part built on craggy and steep rocks, some of which rise perpendicular from the water. And yet the land, both on the north, south, and west, is fruitful and well cultivated. I stood on a little rising near the quay, in a warm, still evening, and exhorted a multitude of people, from all parts, to " seek the Lord, while he may be found." They were all attention ; and most of them met me again at half an hour after four in the morning. I could gladly have spent some days here ; but my stages were fixed : so, on Wednesday, 9, I rode on to York.

Sun. July 8 (London).—After preaching at the chapel, morning and afternoon, I took horse with Mr. P——. We had designed to ride only two or three hours, in order to shorten the next day's journey. But a young man, who overtook us near Kingston, induced us to change our purpose. So we only rested about half an hour at Cobham; and leaving it between nine and ten, rode on softly in a calm, moonshiny night, and about twelve came to Godalming. We took horse again at half an hour past four, and reached Portsmouth about one.

After a little rest, we took a walk round the town, which is regularly fortified; and is, I suppose, the only regular fortification in Great Britain or Ireland. Gosport, Portsmouth, and the Common (which is now all turned into streets), may probably contain half as many people as Bristol: and so civil a people I never saw before in any sea-port town in England.

I preached at half an hour after six, in an open part of the Common, adjoining to the new church. The congregation was large and well-behaved; not one scoffer did I see, nor one trifler. In the morning, Tuesday, 10, I went on board an hoy; and in three hours landed at Cowes, in the Isle of Wight; as far exceeding the Isle of Anglesey, both in pleasantness and fruitfulness, as that exceeds the rocks of Scilly.

We rode straight to Newport, the chief town in the isle, and found a little society in tolerable order. Several of them had found peace with God.

At half an hour after six I preached in the market-place, to a numerous congregation: but they were not so serious as those at Portsmouth. Many children made much noise, and many grown persons were talking aloud, almost all the time I was preaching. It was quite otherwise at five in the morning. There was a large congregation again; and every person therein seemed to know this was the word whereby God would judge them in the last day.

In the afternoon, I walked to Carisbrook castle; or rather, the poor remains of it. It stands upon a solid rock on the top of an hill, and commands a beautiful prospect. There is a well in it, cut quite through the rock, said to be seventy-two yards deep; and another in the citadel, near an hundred. They drew up the water by an ass, which they assured us was sixty years old. But all the stately apartments lie in ruins. Only just enough of them is left, to show the chamber where poor King Charles was confined, and the window through which he attempted to escape.

Cornish Smugglers

On Wednesday, 25, the Stewards met at St. Ives, from the western part of Cornwall. The next day I began examining the society; but I was soon obliged to stop short. I found an accursed thing among them; well-nigh one and all bought or sold uncustomed goods. I therefore delayed speaking to any more till I had met them all together. This I did in the evening, and told them plain, either they must put this abomination away, or they would see my face no more. Friday, 27. They severally promised so to do. So I trust this plague is stayed.

Mon. Nov. 12.—I set out in a chaise for Leigh, having delayed my journey as long as I could. I preached at seven, but was extremely cold all the time, the wind coming strong from a door behind, and another on one side; so that my feet felt just as if I had stood in cold water.

Tues. 13.—The chamber wherein I sat, though with a large fire, was much colder than the garden; so that I could not keep myself tolerably warm, even when I was close to the chimney.   As we rode home on Wednesday, 14, the wind was high and piercing cold, and blew just in our face, so that the open chaise was no defence, but my feet were quite chilled.   When I came home, I had a settled pain in my left breast, a violent cough, and a slow fever; but in a day or two, by following Dr. Fothergill's prescriptions, I found much alteration for the better; and on Sunday, 18, I preached at Spitalfields, and administered the sacrament to a large congregation.

Wesley Writes his Epitaph

Mon. 19.—I retired to Shoreham, and gained strength continually; till about eleven at night, on Wednesday, 21, I was obliged by the cramp to leap out of bed, and continue, for some time, walking up and down the room, though it was a sharp frost.   My cough now returned with greater violence, and that by day as well as by night.

Sat. 24.—I rode home, and was pretty well till night; but my cough was then worse than ever.   My fever returned at the same time, together with the pain in my left breast; so that I should probably have stayed at home on Sunday, 25, had it not been advertised in the public papers, that I would preach a charity sermon at the chapel, both morning and afternoon.   My cough did not interrupt me while I preached in the morning; but it was extremely troublesome while I administered the sacrament.   In the afternoon I consulted my friends, whether I should attempt to preach again or no. They thought I should, as it had been advertised.   I did so; but very few could hear. My fever increased much while I was preaching: however, I ventured to meet the society; and for near an hour my voice and strength were restored, so that I felt neither pain nor weakness.

Mon. 26.—Dr. F.—— told me plain, I must not stay in town a day longer; adding, "If anything does thee good, it must be the country air, with rest, asses' milk, and riding daily." So (not being able to sit an horse) about noon I took coach for Lewisham.

In the evening (not knowing how it might please God to dispose of me), to prevent vile panegyric, I wrote as follows:

𝕳𝖊𝖗𝖊 𝖑𝖎𝖊𝖙𝖍 𝖙𝖍𝖊 𝕭𝖔𝖉𝖞

OF

JOHN WESLEY,

A BRAND PLUCKED OUT OF THE BURNING:

WHO DIED OF A CONSUMPTION IN THE FIFTY-FIRST YEAR

OF HIS AGE,

NOT LEAVING, AFTER HIS DEBTS ARE PAID,

TEN POUNDS BEHIND HIM:

PRAYING,

GOD BE MERCIFUL TO ME, AN UNPROFITABLE SERVANT!

He ordered that this, if any, inscription should be placed on his tombstone.

Wesley his own Doctor

Wed. 28.—I found no change for the better, the medicines which had helped me before, now taking no effect. About noon (the time that some of our brethren in London had set apart for joining in prayer) a thought came into my mind to make an experiment. So I ordered some stone brimstone to be powdered, mixed with the white of an egg, and spread on brown paper, which I applied to my side. The pain ceased in five minutes, the fever in half an hour; and from this hour I began to recover strength. The next day I was able to ride, which I continued to do every day till January 1. Nor did the weather hinder me once; it being always tolerably fair (however it was before) between twelve and one o'clock.

Fri. Dec. 14.—Having finished all the books which I designed to insert in the "Christian Library," I broke through the doctor's order, not to write, and began transcribing a journal for the press; and in the evening I went to prayers with the family, without finding any inconvenience.

Thur. 20.—I felt a gradual increase of strength, till I took a decoction of the bark, which I do not find (such is the pecularity of my constitution) will agree with me in any form whatever. This immediately threw me into a purging, which brought me down again a few days, and quite disappointed me in my design of going out on Christmas Day.

1754. Tues. Jan. 1.—I returned once more to London.

On Wednesday, 2, I set out in the machine and the next afternoon came to Chippenham. Here I took a post-chaise, in which I reached Bristol about eight in the evening.

Fri. 4.—I began drinking the water at the Hot Well, having a lodging at a small distance from it; and on Sunday, 6, I began writing Notes on the New Testament; a work which I should scarce ever have attempted, had I not been so ill as not to be able to travel or preach, and yet so well as to be able to read and write.

Mon. 7.—I went on now in a regular method, rising at my hour, and writing from five to nine at night;

except the time of riding, half an hour for each meal, and the hour between five and six in the evening.

Thur. 31.—My wife desiring to pay the last office to her poor dying child, set out for London, and came a few days before he went home, rejoicing and praising God.

Tues. March 19 (Bristol).—Having finished the rough draught, I began transcribing the Notes on the Gospels.

Tues. 26.—I preached for the first time, after an intermission of four months. What reason have I to praise God, that he does not take the word of his truth utterly out of my mouth!

Wesley Retires to Paddington

Mon. April 1.—We set out in the machine, and the next evening reached the Foundery.

Wed. 3.—I settled all the business I could, and the next morning retired to Paddington. Here I spent some weeks in writing; only going to town on Saturday evenings, and leaving it again on Monday morning.

In my hours of walking I read Dr. Calamy's "Abridgment of Mr. Baxter's Life." What a scene is opened here! In spite of all the prejudice of education, I could not but see that the poor Nonconformists had been used without either justice or mercy; and that many of the Protestant Bishops of King Charles had neither more religion, nor humanity, than the Popish Bishops of Queen Mary.

Mon. 29.—I preached at Sadler's Wells, in what was formerly a play-house. I am glad when it pleases God to take possession of what Satan esteemed his own ground. The place, though large, was extremely crowded; and deep attention sat on every face.

Wed. May 22.—Our Conference began; and the spirit of peace and love was in the midst of us. Before we parted, we all willingly signed an agreement, not to act independently on each other : so that the breach lately made has only united us more closely together than ever.

June 2.—(Being Whit Sunday.) I preached at the Foundery; which I had not done before in the evening; still I have not recovered my whole voice or strength; perhaps I never may : but let me use what I have.

Persecuting the Methodists

Mon. Sept. 9.—I preached at Charlton, a village six miles from Taunton, to a large congregation gathered from the towns and country for many miles round. All the farmers here had some time before entered into a joint engagement to turn all out of their service, and give no work to any, who went to hear a Methodist preacher. But there is no counsel against the Lord. One of the chief of them, Mr. G——, was not long after convinced of the truth, and desired those very men to preach at his house. Many of the other confederates came to hear, whom their servants and labourers gladly followed. So the whole device of Satan fell to the ground; and the word of God grew and prevailed.

Wed. October 2.—I walked to Old Sarum, which, in spite of common sense, without house or inhabitants, still sends two Members to the Parliament. It is a large, round hill, encompassed with a broad ditch, which, it seems, has been of a considerable depth. At the top of it is a cornfield; in the midst of which is another round hill, about two hundred yards in diameter, encompassed with a wall, and a deep ditch. Probably before the invention of cannon, this city was impregnable. Troy was ; but now it is vanished away, and nothing left but " the stones of emptiness."

Thur. 3.—I rode to Reading, and preached in the evening. Observing a warm man near the door (which was once of the society), I purposely bowed to him ; but he made no return. During the first prayer he stood, but sat while we sung. In the sermon his countenance changed, and in a little while he turned his face to the wall. He stood at the second hymn, and then kneeled down. As I came out he catched me by the hand, and dismissed me with a hearty blessing.

Fri. 4.—I came to London. On Monday, 7, I retired to a little place near Hackney, formerly a seat of Bishop Bonner's (how are the times changed ?), and still bearing his name. Here I was as in a College.

Twice a day we joined in prayer. The rest of the day (allowing about an hour for meals, and another for walking before dinner and supper) I spent quietly in my study.

Wesley's Prescriptions

1755. Mon. April 7 (Wednesbury).—I was advised to take the Derbyshire road to Manchester. We baited at an house six miles beyond Lichfield. Observing a woman sitting in the kitchen, I asked, " Are you not well ? " and found she had just been taken ill (being on her journey), with all the symptoms of an approaching pleurisy. She was glad to hear of an easy, cheap, and (almost) infallible remedy—an handful of nettles, boiled a few minutes, and applied warm to the side. While I was speaking to her, an elderly man, pretty well dressed, came in. Upon inquiry, he told us he was travelling, as he could, towards his home near Hounslow, in hopes of agreeing with his creditors, to whom he had surrendered his all. But how to get on he knew not, as he had no money, and had caught a tertian ague. I hope a wise Providence directed this wanderer also, that he might have a remedy for both his maladies.

Mon. 14.—I rode by Manchester (where I preached about twelve) to Warrington. At six in the morning, Tuesday, 15, I preached to a large and serious congregation; and then went on to Liverpool, one of the neatest, best-built towns I have seen in England: I think it is full twice as large as Chester; most of the streets are quite straight. Two thirds of the town, we were informed, have been added within these forty years. If it continue to increase in the same proportion, in forty years more it will nearly equal Bristol. The people in general are the most mild and courteous I ever saw in a seaport town; as indeed appears by their friendly behaviour, not only to the Jews and Papists who live among them, but even to the Methodists (so called). The preaching-house is a little larger than that at Newcastle. It was thoroughly filled at seven in the evening; and the hearts of the whole congregation seemed to be moved before the Lord, and before the presence of his power.

Wesley and the Sunshine

Thur. 24.—We rode in less than four hours the eight miles (so called) to Newell Hay [from Bolton]. Just as I began to preach the sun broke out, and shone exceeding hot on the side of my head. I found, if it continued, I should not be able to speak long, and lifted up my heart to God. In a minute or two it was covered with clouds, which continued till the service was over. Let any who please, call this chance: I call it an answer to prayer.

Fri. 25.—About ten I preached near Todmorden.
The people stood, row above row, on the side of the
mountain. They were rough enough in outward appearance ; but their hearts were as melting wax.

One can hardly conceive anything more delightful
than the vale through which we rode from hence. The
river ran through the green meadows on the right. The
fruitful hills and woods rose on either hand.

At three in the afternoon I preached at Heptonstall,
on the brow of the mountain. The rain began almost
as soon as I began to speak. I prayed that, if God saw
best, it might be stayed, till I had delivered his word.
It was so, and then began again. But we had only a
short stage to Ewood.

Tues. May 6.—Our Conference began at Leeds.
The point on which we desired all the preachers to
speak their minds at large was, " Whether we ought to
separate from the Church ? " Whatever was advanced
on one side or the other was seriously and calmly considered ; and on the third day we were all fully agreed
in that general conclusion—that (whether it was lawful
or not) it was no ways expedient.

Mon. 12.—We rode (my wife and I) to Northaller-
ton.

Wed. 21.—I preached at Nafferton, near Horsley,
about thirteen miles from Newcastle. We rode chiefly
on the new western road, which lies on the old Roman
wall. Some part of this is still to be seen, as are the
remains of most of the towers, which were built a mile
distant from each other, quite from sea to sea. But
where are the men of renown who built them, and who
once made all the land tremble ? Crumbled into dust !
Gone hence, to be no more seen, till the earth shall give
up her dead !

June 2.—We rode to Thirsk, where I met the little society; and then went on to York. The people had been waiting for some time. So I began preaching without delay, and felt no want of strength, though the room was like an oven through the multitude of people.

Sat. 7.—One of the residentiaries sent for Mr. Williamson, who had invited me to preach in his church, and told him, "Sir, I abhor persecution; but if you let Mr. Wesley preach, it will be the worse for you." He desired it nevertheless; but I declined. Perhaps there is a providence in this also. God will not suffer my little remaining strength to be spent on those who will not hear me but in an honourable way.

The Room Was Like an Oven

Sun. 8.—We were at the minster in the morning, and at our parish-church in the afternoon. The same gentleman preached at both; but though I saw him at the church, I did not know I had ever seen him before. In the morning he was all life and motion; in the afternoon he was as quiet as a post. At five in the evening, the rain constrained me to preach in the oven again. The patience of the congregation surprised me. They seemed not to feel the extreme heat, nor to be offended at the close application of those words, "Thou art not far from the kingdom of God."

Mon. 16.—I preached in the evening at Nottingham, and on Thursday afternoon reached London. From a deep sense of the amazing work which God has of late years wrought in England, I preached in the evening on those words (Psalm cxlvii. 20), "He hath not dealt so with any nation"; no, not even with Scotland or New-England. In both these God has indeed made bare his arm; yet not in so astonishing a manner as among us.